Afro-Americans in Pittsburgh

Afro-Americans in Pittsburgh

The Residential Segregation of a People

Joe T. Darden
Michigan State University

Lexington Books
D.C. Heath and Company
Lexington, Massachusetts
Toronto   London

Library of Congress Cataloging in Publication Data

Darden, Joe T.
  Afro-Americans in Pittsburgh.

  Bibliography: p.
  1. Negroes—Pittsburgh. 2. Discrimination in housing—Pittsburgh. 3. Negroes—Housing. I. Title.
F159.P6D18   301.45'042   73-1232
ISBN 0-669-86728-4

Published simultaneously in Canada.

Printed in the United States of America.

International Standard Book Number: 0-669-86728-4

Library of Congress Catalog Card Number: 73-1232

To Sophia

Contents

List of Figures

List of Tables

Preface

If racial residential segregation did not exist, such controversial phenomena as "school busing" would not be an issue. But residential segregation between blacks and whites is a fact of American life. Furthermore, place of residence is the cause, not a symptom, of segregation in other aspects of American life. Its importance, therefore, cannot be overemphasized. Yet American society continues to ignore this problem. Until the pattern of racial residential segregation is adequately confronted and altered, future racial conflict in American cities is inevitable.

The present analysis avoids racial rhetoric. Instead, a serious, in-depth look is taken at black residential segregation. How much segregation exists, the changes over time, and the causes are quantitatively examined. It is hoped that such findings will lead to a better understanding and to more action on the part of those who are concerned with improving race relations.

Several individuals have aided in the preparation of this study, and to them I am grateful. Sincere appreciation is extended to Hibberd V.B. Kline, Jr., Philip Vernon, and Oswald Schmidt of the Department of Geography and Donald Henderson of the Department of Sociology, University of Pittsburgh.

Much of the data on racial discrimination could not have been obtained without the assistance of David Washington, former executive director of the Pittsburgh Commission on Human Relations. I am greatly in his debt.

I am indebted also to the University of Pittsburgh Social Science Information Center for assistance in computer programming. Sincere appreciation is extended to the director, Philip Sidel, and to members of the staff, Ruth Sabean and Richard Travis. In addition, I would like to thank Howard Ziegler for his cartographic assistance. Most of the writing of this work was done at the University of Chicago. Appreciation is extended to Brian J.L. Berry of the Department of Geography for his helpful comments.

1

Introduction

Residential segregation is the foundation for segregation in other aspects of society, such as public schools, churches, and recreation. Residential segregation can be said to exist wherever the residential distribution of the white population differs from that of the black population, whatever the amount of the difference. Thus, in any study of segregation the important question is usually not whether an area is segregated but how much it is segregated.

Although residential segregation is a spatial phenomenon, few geographers have studied it.[1] The majority of studies have been conducted by sociologists.[2] Most studies of residential segregation have focused primarily on either the degree of segregation or the relationship between segregation and economic inequality. Few have explicitly considered the effect of racial discrimination in housing on residential segregation. One aim of this study is to expand our understanding of residential segregation to encompass the role of racial discrimination.

More specifically, this study has two main objectives: (1) to measure the spatial dimensions and spatial dynamics of residential segregation of Afro-Americans in Pittsburgh from 1930 to 1970; and (2) to identify in both economic and discriminatory terms, the causes of these spatial dimensions and spatial dynamics. "Spatial dimensions" here refers to the magnitude, or amount, of segregation that exists and "spatial dynamics" to the changes that have occurred in residential segregation over time and space. The terms Afro-American, black, and Negro are used interchangeably in this study to refer to Americans of African descent.

In Pittsburgh, this study is confined to the incorporated city. Of the city's total population, 520,117 in 1970, more than 20 percent are black.[3] A northern city was chosen because residential separation by race has much more significance in northern cities than in many southern cities. In fact, residential segregation serves a special function in the North. In the South the strong taboos against social equality and intimate associations between whites and blacks have eliminated much of the significance of separate black residential areas. The place for blacks within the society is well-defined within the social arena. In the North, where social status or "place" for blacks within the society has not been as clearly defined, residence in a particular residential area is perceived as an indicator of social status. Therefore, racial residential separation is very important.[4]

The following hypotheses are tested: (1) the residential segregation of

1

Afro-Americans in Pittsburgh since 1930 (a) remained at a high level (above 50 percent according to the Gini index described later) between 1930 and 1970 and (b) increased continuously over that period; and (2) the high level of residential segregation in Pittsburgh has been caused not by housing cost inequality but by racial discrimination in housing.

The remainder of this chapter is devoted to a review of data sources and methodology and a brief discussion of the development of Pittsburgh's black communities. Chapter 2 describes the spatial dimensions and spatial dynamics of residential segregation of Afro-Americans in Pittsburgh from 1930-1970. Quantitative data and statistical analysis demonstrate that Pittsburgh remained from 70.5 to 75.7 percent segregated over the study period. It is also demonstrated, however, that the spatial dynamics, or changes in residential segregation, were not consistent from 1930-1970. There were decades of increase in segregation and decades of decrease. Finally, the chapter examines the extent and direction of racial transition within census tracts over the forty-year period. Chapter 3 focuses on the influence of housing cost on racial residential segregation and demonstrates statistically that housing cost cannot explain the observed high level of segregation in Pittsburgh. Only a small portion of the segregation can be attributed to housing cost inequality between the races. Chapter 4 demonstrates that racial discrimination in housing is a primary cause of residential segregation. Finally, Chapter 5 summarizes the study's major conclusions.

Data and Methodology

Data on residential segregation in Pittsburgh were obtained from United States census tract statistics (see Bibliography for full citations), the files of the Pittsburgh Commission on Human Relations, the files of the United States District Court for Western Pennsylvania, and interviews with selected real estate brokers of Pittsburgh.

Index of Segregation

The index of segregation described below and the segregation curve (Lorenz curve) to be discussed in the next section were used to measure the degree of segregation by census tracts. The index of segregation[5] can be expressed mathematically as:

$$S = x_i - y_i$$

where x_i is the percent of the city's white population residing in a given census tract and y_i is the percent of the city's black population residing in the same census tract. The derived value indicates the percentage of either race that would have to move into or out of the tract to make the percentages equal. For example, in Table 1-1, the segregation index S in tract 1-A is 1.8 percent, indicating an uneven spatial distribution of the two populations, with a 1.8 percent racial deficit—in this case a deficit of blacks since the percent of the city's white population is larger than the percent of the city's black population. To eliminate the deficit, either 1.8 percent of the city's black population would have to move into tract 1-A or 1.8 percent of the city's white population would have to move out of the tract. Similar relocations would be required to bring about an even distribution among the remaining census tracts. Using the formula given above, each tract could be identified as one of the following: (1) a white segregated area, that is, a tract which has a higher percentage of the city's white population than of the city's black population; (2) a black segregated area, or a tract where the percentage is higher for the black population; or (3) a nonsegregated area, a tract in which the two percentages are equal. Maps could be constructed, indicating areas in each category and their percent racial deficits (S in the formula).

The reader is reminded that the segregation index numbers or percent racial deficits, like any index numbers, are statistical tools. They are useful for spatial analysis, but they do not reflect the "reality" of segregation any more than I.Q. scores reflect the "reality" of intelligence, the cost-of-living index the "reality" of the cost of living, or a pollution index the "reality" of pollution.[6] Indexes of segregation are of practical use, however, in that they provide social planners and other concerned citizens with precise information as to how close a city or area is to certain desirable or undesirable points. For example if it is a desired goal of the people of Pittsburgh to have 0.0 percent segregation, or no segregation, in every census tract, the indexes of segregation can show them how close Pittsburgh is to that goal.

A map of the data in Table 1-1 would show tract 1-A as a white segregated

Table 1-1
Measurement of Segregation Among Census Tracts for Hypothetical City

Tracts	Whites as Percent of Total Whites (x_i)	Percent Racial Deficit ($x_i - y_i$)	Blacks as Percent of Total Blacks (Y_i)
1-A	34.2	1.8	32.4
1-B	5.7	5.7	11.4
2-A	2.2	1.5	3.7
2-B	46.3	8.4	37.9
3-A	10.1	0.0	10.1
3-B	1.5	3.1	4.6

area with a racial deficit of blacks in the amount of 1.8 percent. To make tract 1-A a nonsegregated area, with a percent racial deficit of 0.0, either 1.8 percent of the city's black population would have to move into the tract or 1.8 percent of the city's white population would have to move out. Tract 1-B is a black segregated area with a racial deficit of whites in the amount of 5.7 percent. Thus tract 1-B is more segregated than tract 1-A. To make tract 1-B a nonsegregated area, either 5.7 percent of the city's white population would have to move in or 5.7 percent of the city's black population would have to move out. Tract 2-A is less segregated than either 1-A or 1-B; it is a black segregated area with a deficit of whites in the amount of 1.5 percent. Tract 2-B is a white segregated area and the most segregated tract in the city with a percent racial deficit of 8.4 percent. Tract 3-A is a nonsegregated area. Its percent racial deficit is already 0.0, requiring no movement of the races. Finally, tract 3-B is a black segregated area with a deficit of whites in the amount of 3.1 percent. Appendix A provides further examples using actual tracts in Pittsburgh.

Several past studies[7] of residential segregation have relied solely on summary measures of segregation, such as the degree of segregation for an entire city, without any breakdown into smaller areas. Mapping the degree of segregation in each census tract enables us to observe the pattern of segregation within the larger area studied and also to compare and observe spatial changes in this pattern over time.

Gini Index and Lorenz Curve

The Gini index and Lorenz curve were used to measure the degree of segregation for the incorporated city of Pittsburgh as a whole. Although there is little or no mathematical difference between the Gini index and the segregation index (if used as a summary measure),[8] the Gini index was preferred because of the additional advantage of visual comparison made possible by the Lorenz curve.[9] Computation of the Gini index and Lorenz curve proceeded as follows.[10] Census tracts were arranged in order from high to low on the basis of the percentage of their population that is black, and a black percentage cumulative for each tract was computed. Then a white cumulative percentage for each tract was computed. The white cumulative percentages were then plotted against the black cumulative percentages to derive a Lorenz or segregation curve.

The rationale of the Lorenz or segregation curve is as follows: If whites and blacks were evenly distributed, every census tract would have equal percentages of Pittsburgh's total population of blacks and whites, making the cumulative percentages of these groups equal with a Gini index equal to 0.00. The Lorenz or segregation curve would be a straight line at a 45-degree angle. On the other hand, if the spatial distribution of whites and blacks were completely uneven, with each census tract either all white or all black, the Lorenz or segregation curve would be coincident with the axes and the Gini index would be 1.00. The size of the Gini index indicates the amount of segregation.

Technical Limitations of Method
of Measuring Segregation

A shortcoming of the segregation and Gini indexes is that they are sensitive to the size of areal units used.[11] The smaller the spatial units, the greater the possible value of the segregation or Gini index. For example, let us assume that a Gini index value based on census tracts is 50.0. A Gini index value based on wards would not be greater than 50.0 and would probably be less. On the other hand, a Gini index value based on city blocks would not be less than 50.0 and would probably be greater.

The choice of spatial unit to measure residential segregation must be a function of the problem under investigation and of data availability; there is no such thing as "the best spatial unit." For this study, which involves mapping and analyzing racial change within the city, census tracts were more appropriate than either wards or blocks. Their major limitation was that the degree and magnitude of segregation by block could not be determined. The segregation index takes into account only differences in the percentage of the two racial groups in each census tract within the city and reveals nothing about intratract distributions. Thus it is possible that in a tract classified as nonsegregated, with equal percentages of the city's black and white populations, there could still be total segregation by block.

During the period 1930-1970, there were some minor revisions in Pittsburgh's tract boundaries, plus some annexations. The revisions were too slight to affect the Gini indexes obtained, and since the populations of the annexed areas were small, even these changes probably had only negligible effect on the results. Thus no adjustments were made in this study for boundary revisions, and tracts annexed during a given decade.

Multiple Correlation and Regression of
Percentage Black and Housing Cost

To measure the influence of housing cost on racial residential segregation, percent black by census tracts was regressed against four economic variables. These variables, which are defined in Chapter 3, were percent high housing value, percent low housing value, percent high rent and percent low rent. The analysis covers the period 1940-1970, since data prior to 1940 were not available.

The reason for measuring economic status by the value of a resident's house or the rent he pays instead of by his income is that his income does not precisely reflect his ability to pay for housing. For example, let us assume that a given white individual earns $8,000 a year and a given black individual $6,000. Both might pay $95.00 per month rent for a house. This phenomenon, in which blacks are denied economic equality in certain areas (income) but forced to be equal in others (cost of housing) is common in Pittsburgh and throughout the United States. Even at equal levels of education and occupation, blacks, on the average, earn less income than whites. This, together with the higher proportion of blacks at lower levels of education and occupation, leaves no doubt that racial economic inequality in terms of income is a fact of American life. Pittsburgh is no exception. However the fact that blacks earn less income than whites does not necessarily indicate that blacks pay less than whites for housing. To measure the influence of housing cost on racial residential segregation, it is therefore much more meaningful and more precise to focus on the cost of the housing than on the income of the occupants.[12]

Percentage of Complaints of Racial
Discrimination in Housing

The analysis demonstrating that racial discrimination in housing is a major cause of racial residential segregation is limited to the period 1959-1970 because of lack of data prior to mid-1959. For the years studied, percentages of complaints of racial discrimination were related to (1) type of discriminator, (2) type of property, (3) type of alleged violation, and (4) type of community. The use of complaints as indicators of discrimination has the drawback that it leads to underestimation of the amount of discrimination that exist, since many incidents of discrimination go unrecorded.

Development of Pittsburgh's Black Communities

Continuous migration to a limited number of heavily black populated census tracts and natural increase in these tracts have been the components in the formation and expansion of "black ghettos" in Pittsburgh. Lured by the prospect of higher wages and opportunity for social betterment, black migrants from the South crowded into Pittsburgh early in this century to such an extent that between 1910 and 1930, their numbers increased 93 percent.[13] Most of these migrants came from the states of West Virginia, Virginia, North Carolina, South Carolina, Georgia, and Alabama[14]—the latter, in some cases because Birmingham was thought of as "the Pittsburgh of the South."[15] After the Great Depression, another major wave of migration of Afro-Americans began. The demand for industrial labor contributed to an increase of 38,675 Afro-Americans from 1940 to 1960. Migration and natural increase combined raised the total black population from 54,983 in 1930 to 100,692 in 1960, the largest three-decade increase in the history of Pittsburgh.

Figure 1-1 shows Pittsburgh's communities. From 1930 to 1970, at least two-thirds of the black population of Pittsburgh was concentrated in three areas, namely the communities[16] of the Hill District, Homewood Brushton, and East Liberty, although in recent years the black population outside these communities has increased.

The growing number of blacks in limited areas has created a demand for housing that far exceeds the supply. To accommodate the increasing numbers, many one-family dwellings have been converted into multiple dwellings by splitting small rooms into smaller rooms, and overcrowding has led to deterioration of the limited housing available. Since it has been extremely difficult for blacks to secure housing outside segregated black areas, landlords and real estate brokers have been under no pressure to see that repairs are made. Exploiting the great need for more housing, they have been able to rent or sell almost any kind of house, regardless of quality. Lower-quality housing for blacks than for whites has become the rule, and blacks have been forced to pay higher rents than whites for housing of the same quality or equal rents for lower-quality housing.[17] This phenomenon has been described by Rose as the "color tax," or the price that a resident pays for being black and living in America.[18] The fact that many blacks could afford housing in white residential areas has been well documented.[19]

The present study of Pittsburgh provides clear evidence that Afro-American residential segregation is due to racial discrimination and not simply to housing cost inequality. Therefore, upward economic mobility by blacks will not necessarily result in outward spatial mobility. So long as racial discrimination in housing continues, the level of residential segregation in Pittsburgh will not be substantially reduced. Thus, if causes of racial residential segregation are to be understood and solutions to the problem found, more attention must be given to the coercive and manipulative behavior of whites, both institutional and individual.

Notes

1. Of interest are Richard Morrill, "The Negro Ghetto: Problems and Alternatives," GEOGRAPHICAL REVIEW 55 (1965), 339-361; and Harold M. Rose, "The Development of an Urban Subsystem: The Case of the Negro Ghetto," ANNALS OF THE ASSOCIATION OF AMERICAN GEOGRAPHERS 60 (1970): 1-17.

2. Typical studies are Wendell Bell and Ernest M. Willis, "The Segregation of Negroes in American Cities," SOCIAL AND ECONOMIC STUDIES 6 (1957); Ernest W. Burgess, "Residential Segregation in American Cities," ANNALS OF THE AMERICAN ACADEMY OF POLITICAL AND SOCIAL SCIENCE 140

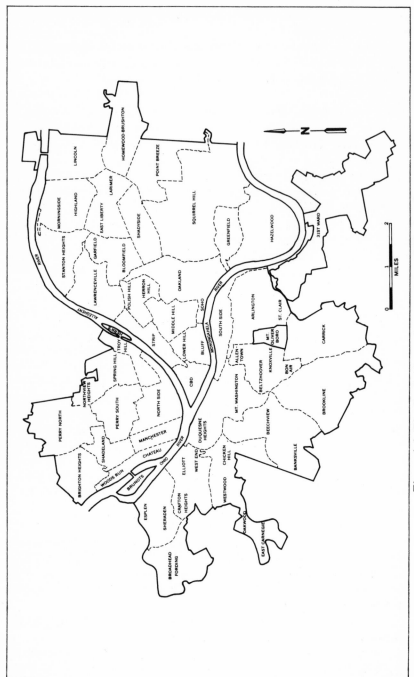

Figure 1-1. The Study Area: Communities of Pittsburgh

(November 1928): 105-115; Karl E. Taeuber, "The Effect of Income Redistribution on Racial Residential Segregation," URBAN AFFAIRS QUARTERLY 4 (September 1958): 5-14.

3. See U.S., Department of Commerce, Bureau of the Census, UNITED STATES CENSUS OF POPULATION: 1970, GENERAL POPULATION CHARACTERISTICS, Advance Report, Pennsylvania.

4. See Bertram W. Doyle, THE ETIQUETTE OF RACE RELATIONS IN THE SOUTH (Chicago: University of Chicago Press, 1937), p. 172; also St. Clair Drake and Horace R. Cayton, BLACK METROPOLIS: A STUDY OF NEGRO LIFE IN A NORTHERN CITY (New York: Harcourt, Brace, 1945), pp. 174, 759.

5. When used as a summary measure, the index of segregation is the same as the index of dissimilarity devised and discussed by Duncan and Duncan. See Otis D. Duncan and Beverly Duncan, "A Methodological Analysis of Segregation Indexes," AMERICAN SOCIOLOGICAL REVIEW 20 (April 1955): 210-17.

6. See Nathan Kantrowitz, "Ethnic and Racial Segregation in the New York Metropolis, 1960," AMERICAN JOURNAL OF SOCIOLOGY 74 (1969): 686.

7. See Alma F. Taeuber and Karl E. Taeuber, "The Negro as an Immigrant Group: Recent Trends in Racial and Ethnic Segregation in Chicago," AMERICAN JOURNAL OF SOCIOLOGY 69 (1964): 374-82; Donald O. Cowgill, "Trends in Residential Segregation of Nonwhites in American Cities, 1940-1950," AMERICAN SOCIOLOGICAL REVIEW 21 (February, 1958): 43-47; Stanley Lieberson, "The Impact of Residential Segregation on Ethnic Assimilation," SOCIAL FORCES 40 (1961): 52-57; Karl E. Taeuber, "Residential Segregation," SCIENTIFIC AMERICAN 213 (1965): 12-19; and Kantrowitz, "Ethnic and Racial Segregation in the New York Metropolis."

8. For a detailed discussion of the correlation between the Gini index and segregation index see Julius A. Jahn, Calvin F. Schmid, and Clarence Schrag, "The Measurement of Ecological Segregation," AMERICAN SOCIOLOGICAL REVIEW 12 (June 1947): 293-303; and Duncan and Duncan, "Methodological Analysis of Segregation Indexes." Also Maurice G. Kendall, THE ADVANCED THEORY OF STATISTICS (London: Griffin & Co., 3rd ed., 1947), Vol. 1, Ch. 2.

9. For a discussion of the initial introduction of the Lorenz curve as a measure, see O.M. Lorenz, "Methods of Measuring the Concentration of Wealth," PUBLICATIONS OF THE AMERICAN STATISTICAL ASSOCIATION, New Series, 9 (1904-1905): 209-19. See also Edgar M. Hoover, "The Measurement of Industrial Localization," REVIEW OF ECONOMICS AND STATISTICS 18 (November 1936): 162-171.

10. A computer program from the University of Pittsburgh Social Science Information Center was used to compute the Gini index and Lorenz curve.

11. This limitation applies to all measures of spatial distribution which are based on areal units. For a detailed discussion and illustration of this short-

coming, see Otis D. Duncan, Ray P. Cuzzart, and Beverly Duncan, STATISTI-
CAL GEOGRAPHY: PROBLEMS IN ANALYZING AREAL DATA (Glencoe,
Illinois: The Free Press, 1961). See also Donald O. Cowgill and Mary Cowgill,
"An Index of Segregation Based on Block Statistics," AMERICAN SOCIOLOGI-
CAL REVIEW 16 (December 1951): 825-31; and Josephine Williams, "Another
Commentary on the So-called Segregation Indices," AMERICAN SOCIOLOGI-
CAL REVIEW 13 (June 1948): 298-303; also Jack P. Gibbs, "Some Measures of
the Spatial Distribution and Redistribution of Urban Phenomena" in URBAN
RESEARCH METHODS, ed. by Jack P. Gibbs (Princeton: D. Von Nostrand Co.,
Inc., 1961), pp. 235-51; and John R. Wright, "Some Measures of Distribution,"
ANNALS OF THE ASSOCIATION OF AMERICAN GEOGRAPHERS, 27
(December 1937): 177-211. A measure which is relatively independent of the
spatial unit used has been devised by Roberto Bachi, STATISTICAL ANALYSIS
OF GEOGRAPHICAL SERIES (Jerusalem: Hebrew University and Israel Central
Bureau of Statistics, 1957). The measure has been further illustrated by Douglas
B. Lee, "Analysis and Description of Residential Segregation" (unpublished
M.A. thesis, Cornell University, 1966). The measure is referred to as a
centrographic technique. While the values are affected only incidentally by the
type of spatial unit employed, generally, the smaller the spatial unit, the more
precise the measure. See Walter Isard, METHODS OF REGIONAL ANALYSIS:
AN INTRODUCTION TO REGIONAL SCIENCE (New York: John Wiley &
Sons, Inc., 1960), p. 264.

12. Wallace used income as a variable and a segregation index method in his
study of black concentration in Chicago. He found that *low* income as a
locational factor could account for less than half of the concentration (segregation) of blacks in Chicago. See David A. Wallace, "Residential Concentration
of Negroes in Chicago" (unpublished Ph.D. dissertation, Harvard University,
1953), p. 195.

13. Elsie Witchen, TUBERCULOSIS AND THE NEGRO IN PITTSBURGH
(Pittsburgh: Tuberculosis League of Pittsburgh, 1934), p. 2.

14. Alonzo G. Moron and F.F. Stephen, "The Negro Population in Pittsburgh and Allegheny County," THE SOCIAL RESEARCH BULLETIN 1 (April
20, 1933): 2.

15. Abraham Epstein, THE NEGRO MIGRANT IN PITTSBURGH (Pittsburgh: University of Pittsburgh Press, 1918), p. 24.

16. A community is an area of common living which is defined according to
the interests or characteristics of the people living in it, and in which the people
have the sense of being a unit. See John T. Zadrozny, DICTIONARY OF
SOCIAL SCIENCE (Washington, D.C.: Public Affairs Press, 1959); also G.A.
Hillery, "Definitions of Community: Areas of Agreement," RURAL SOCI-
OLOGY 20 (1955): 119.

17. Commonwealth of Pennsylvania, Department of Welfare, NEGRO SUR-
VEY OF PENNSYLVANIA (Harrisburg, 1928), pp. 35-37.

18. Harold M. Rose, SOCIAL PROCESSES IN THE CITY: RACE AND URBAN RESIDENTIAL CHOICE, Commission on College Geography, Resource Paper No. 6 (Washington, D.C.: Association of American Geographers, 1969), p. 2; see also Bernard Frieden, THE FUTURE OF OLD NEIGHBORHOODS (Cambridge: MIT Press, 1964); also Chester Rapkin, "Price Discrimination Against Negroes in the Rental Housing Market," ESSAYS IN URBAN LAND ECONOMICS (Los Angeles: University of California Real Estate Research Program, 1966); and David McIntire, RESIDENCE AND RACE (Berkeley, University of California Press, 1960).

19. See Richard Langendorf, "Residential Desegregation Potential," JOURNAL OF THE AMERICAN INSTITUTE OF PLANNERS (March 1969), pp. 90-95; also Rose, SOCIAL PROCESSES IN THE CITY, pp. 20-21.

2

The Spatial Patterns and Spatial Dynamics of Residential Segregation, 1930-1970

Having traced the development of Pittsburgh's black communities, we will now examine the pattern of residential segregation of Afro-Americans in that city from 1930-1970. This chapter seeks to answer the following questions: (1) Has racial residential segregation in Pittsburgh remained at a high level from 1930 to 1970? (2) Has the trend in residential segregation in Pittsburgh been one of continuous increase through time? (3) What census tracts have been more segregated than others? (4) How have census tracts changed in racial composition?

In this study a high level of segregation is arbitrarily defined as a Gini index above 50 percent. That is, a city has a high level of segregation if more than half its population of either race would have to change residence to make it 0.00 percent segregated, or nonsegregated.

1930-1940

In 1930 the level of segregation between blacks and whites in Pittsburgh was 71.6 percent, as shown in Figure 2-1. Figure 2-2 shows the amount of segregation in each census tract. The black population was highly segregated, particularly in the Hill District. The degree to which it was segregated in each census tract may be determined by examining the percent racial deficit, or segregation index, for each tract. The higher the percent racial deficit, the greater the segregation. Of the city's black segregated areas, the highest segregated tract in 1930, located in the Hill District, had an 8.03 percent racial deficit. Thus 8.03 percent of the black population of Pittsburgh would have to move out of this tract or 8.03 percent of the city's white population would have to move into it to change it to a nonsegregated tract. The lowest segregated tract among the black segregated areas had a percent racial deficit of 0.01. The highest segregated tract among the white segregated areas had a percent racial deficit of only 1.84, indicating that the white population was more widely distributed than the black population. Only one census tract (located adjacent a black area) was nonsegregated in 1930.

By 1940, segregation of Afro-Americans in Pittsburgh had increased 3.3 percentage points to 74.9 percent (Figure 2-3). The most segregated tract was again located in the Hill district, this time with a racial deficit of 10.69 percent (Figure 2-4), illustrating the increase in segregation since 1930 in the already highly segregated black census tracts.

13

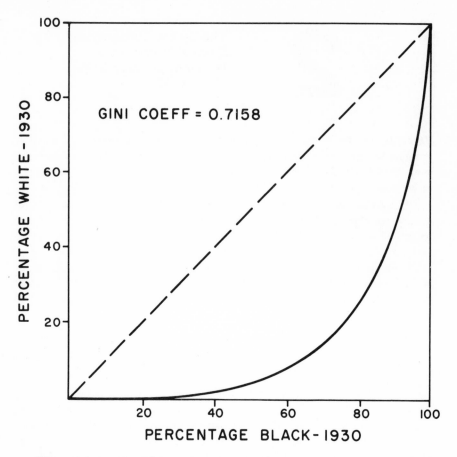

Figure 2-1. Residential Segregation of Afro-Americans in Pittsburgh, 1930

In terms of our classification of census tracts as black segregated, white segregated, or nonsegregated, a tract can experience racial change in six different ways: (1) black to white, (2) black to nonsegregated, (3) white to black, (4) white to nonsegregated, (5) nonsegregated to black, and (6) nonsegregated to white. During the decade 1930-1940 thirteen tracts in Pittsburgh experienced racial change, as summarized in Table 2-1. Five tracts changed from black segregated to white segregated. In other words, in 1930 these five tracts or areas had a deficit of whites, but by 1940 they had changed to the extent that there was a deficit of blacks. Previous studies have indicated that the direction of racial change has usually been in the opposite direction, from white to black.[1] However, only four tracts changed from white to black. Thus, there was an

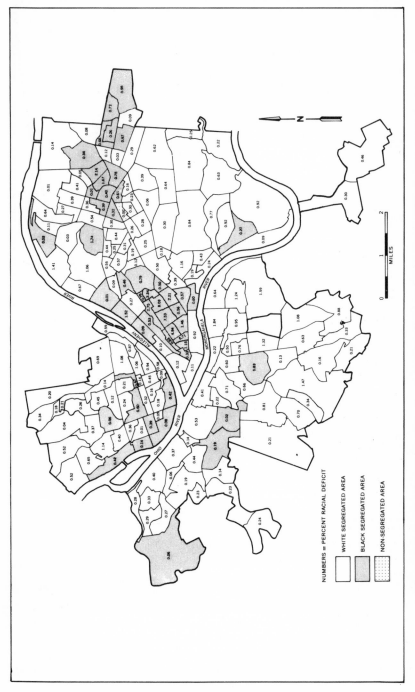

Figure 2-2. Spatial Pattern of Afro-American Residential Segregation in Pittsburgh, 1930

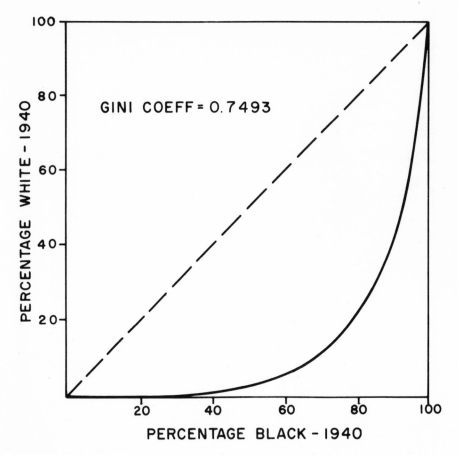

Figure 2-3. Residential Segregation of Afro-Americans in Pittsburgh, 1940

increased concentration of the black population in a limited number of already segregated black census tracts.

Such a trend ultimately leads to what has been called a "piling up process."[2] This process occurs when tracts that have become virtually all black (97.5 percent or more) continue to increase their black populations, resulting in higher population densities, partitioning of dwelling units into smaller units, and increased room crowding.[3] Such are some of the physical components in black ghetto formation.

Only two tracts changed from black to nonsegregated and only one from white to nonsegregated. The latter was a tract located in the Morningside-Highland community adjacent the Allegheny River. No tracts changed from nonsegre-

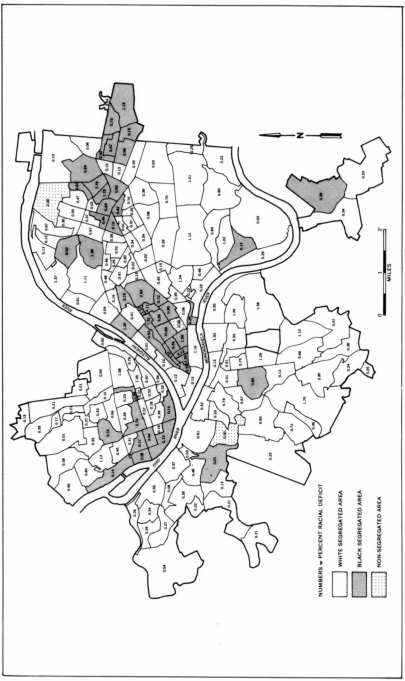

NUMBERS = PERCENT RACIAL DEFICIT

WHITE SEGREGATED AREA

BLACK SEGREGATED AREA

NON-SEGREGATED AREA

Figure 2-4. Spatial Pattern of Afro-American Residential Segregation in Pittsburgh, 1940

Table 2-1
Distribution of Percent Racial Deficit Among Census Tracts Experiencing Racial Change, 1930-1940

Percent Racial Deficit in 1930	Community	Type of Racial Change
0.01	East Liberty-Larimer	Black to White
0.03	Stanton Heights	Black to White
0.06	Broadhead Fording	Black to White
0.09	Strip	Black to White
0.57	Middle Hill	Black to White
0.02	Beechview-Banksville	Black to Nonsegregated
0.56	Middle Hill	Black to Nonsegregated
0.01	Manchester	White to Black
0.03	Stanton Heights	White to Black
0.05	East Liberty-Larimer	White to Black
0.09	Homewood-Brushton	White to Black
0.01	Morningside-Highland	White to Nonsegregated
0.00	Shadyside	Nonsegregated to White

gated to black and only one changed from nonsegregated to white. As Table 2-1 shows, racial change occurred only in tracts that were less than one percent segregated in 1930.

1940-1950

By 1950 Afro-American residential segregation had increased to 75.7 percent (Figure 2-5), an increase of 0.8 percentage points. The most segregated census tract was still located in the Hill District, with a racial deficit of 8.18 percent (Figure 2-6), a decrease from the 1940 maximum level of 10.69 percent.

During the decade 1940-1950 only seven tracts experienced racial change, and all had racial deficits of less than one percent (Table 2-2). Three tracts changed from black to white. No tracts changed from black to nonsegregated. Only two tracts changed from white to black. No tracts changed from white to nonsegregated. One tract changed from nonsegregated to black, and one tract changed from nonsegregated to white.

1950-1960

Pittsburgh reached its peak level of residential segregation in the decade 1940-1950. From 1950 to 1960, there was a very slight decrease in residential

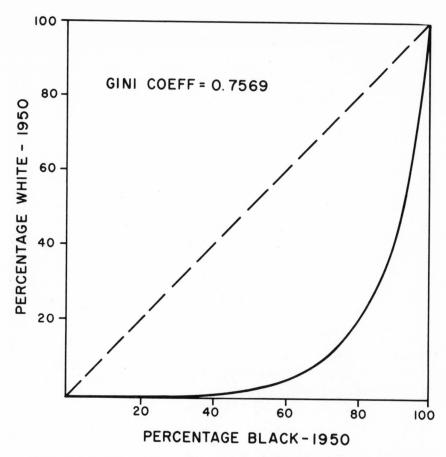

Figure 2-5. Residential Segregation of Afro-Americans in Pittsburgh, 1950

segregation, by 2.8 percentage points, to 72.9 percent (Figure 2-7). The most segregated census tract was still located in the Hill District, with a racial deficit of 5.61 percent (Figure 2-8), down from 8.18 percent in 1950.

During 1950 to 1960 ten tracts experienced racial change, all of which had racial deficits of less than one percent (Table 2-3). Two tracts changed from black to white. Only one tract changed from black to nonsegregated. Six tracts changed from white to black. No tracts changed from white to nonsegregated and no tracts changed from nonsegregated to black. However one tract changed from nonsegregated to white.

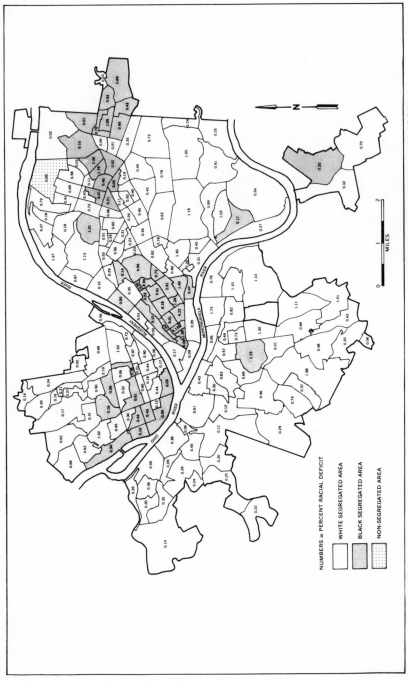

Figure 2-6. Spatial Pattern of Afro-American Residential Segregation in Pittsburgh, 1950

Table 2-2

Distribution of Percent Racial Deficit Among Census Tracts Experiencing Racial Change, 1940-1950

Percent Racial Deficit in 1940	Community	Type of Racial Change
0.01	East Liberty-Larimer	Black to White
0.01	Chicken Hill	Black to White
0.02	Stanton Heights	Black to White
0.06	Perry South	White to Black
0.08	Middle Hill	White to Black
0.00	Middle Hill	Nonsegregated to Black
0.00	Beechview	Nonsegregated to White

1960-1970

From 1960 to 1970 Afro-American residential segregation again decreased slightly, by 2.4 percentage points. The Gini index in 1970 was 70.5 percent (Figure 2-9). While most tracts in the Hill District decreased in segregation, most tracts in Homewood-Brushton increased in segregation. By 1970, the most segregated tract in the city was no longer located in the Hill District but in Homewood-Brushton (Figure 2-10). This tract had the lowest racial deficit of the most segregated tracts over the four decades—4.34 percent.

One of the most striking changes that occurred from 1960-1970 was the evolution of additional black segregated areas (Figure 2-10). This is revealed by the relatively high amount of segregation in tracts located in Northview Heights and the St. Clair Village communities. These are areas of Public Housing.

During the decade 1960-1970 fifteen tracts experienced racial change, all of which had percent racial deficits of less than one percent (Table 2-4). As residential segregation in the city declined, racial change from black to white increased. Five tracts changed in this direction, the highest number since the decade of 1930-1940 when residential segregation was at its second lowest level, 71.6 percent. Eight tracts changed from white to black, one from white to nonsegregated, and one from black to nonsegregated. No tracts changed from nonsegregated to either black or white.

Summary and Conclusions

The above results show that Pittsburgh did have a high level of residential segregation over the forty-year study period. Gini indices ranged from 70.5 to 75.7 percent, as shown in Figure 2-11. The results disprove the hypothesis that segregation has been increasing in Pittsburgh since 1930. Segregation increased in

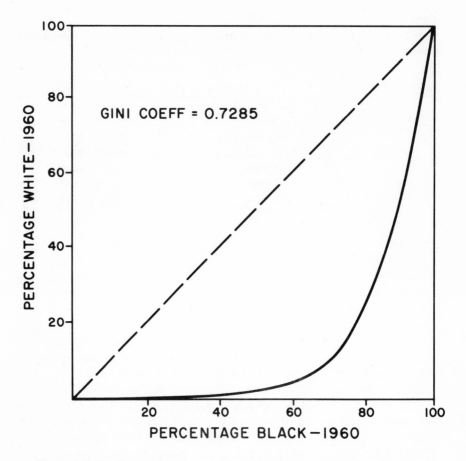

Figure 2-7. Residential Segregation of Afro-Americans in Pittsburgh, 1960

the first two decades studied but decreased in the last two. In 1930, when the study begins, segregation was at a high level. From 1930 to 1940 there was an increase in segregation of 3.3 percentage points. The decade 1940-1950 witnessed another, smaller, increase. However, from 1950 to 1960 there was a small decrease in residential segregation of 2.8 percentage points. This downward trend continued in 1960-1970 with a 2.4 percent decrease.

The findings by census tract show that from 1930 to 1960 the most segregated tracts in the city were in the Hill District. However, due to continued increases in residential segregation of most tracts in Homewood-Brushton and slight decreases in residential segregation of most tracts in the Hill District, tracts in the former community became the most segregated by 1970.

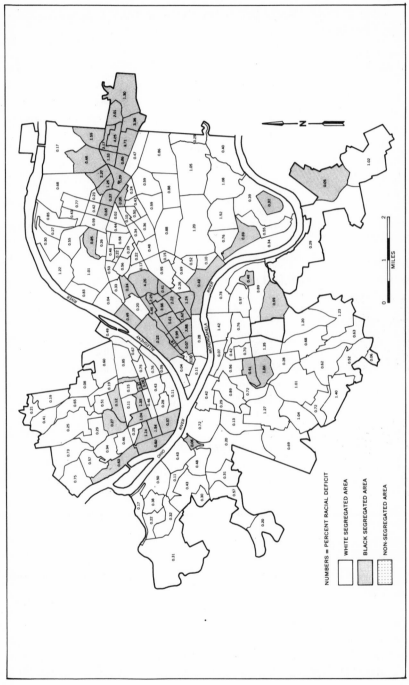

NUMBERS = PERCENT RACIAL DEFICIT

WHITE SEGREGATED AREA

BLACK SEGREGATED AREA

NON-SEGREGATED AREA

Figure 2-8. Spatial Pattern of Afro-American Residential Segregation in Pittsburgh, 1960

Table 2-3

Distribution of Percent Racial Deficit Among Census Tracts Experiencing Racial Change, 1950-1960

Percent Racial Deficit in 1950	Community	Type of Racial Change
0.03	Northside	Black to White
0.21	East Liberty-Larimer	Black to White
0.09	CBD	Black to Nonsegregated
0.01	Strip	White to Black
0.01	Homewood-Brushton	White to Black
0.06	Homewood-Brushton	White to Black
0.06	West End	White to Black
0.21	Perry South	White to Black
0.31	Soho	White to Black
0.00	Morningside-Highland	Nonsegregated to White

Table 2-4

Distribution of Percent Racial Deficit Among Census Tracts Experiencing Racial Change, 1960-1970

Percent Racial Deficit in 1960	Community	Type of Racial Change
0.05	31st Ward	Black to White
0.05	Shadyside	Black to White
0.07	Lower Hill	Black to White
0.24	Polish Hill	Black to White
0.65	East Liberty	Black to White
0.60	Chateau	Black to Nonsegregated
0.08	Northview Heights	White to Black
0.10	Oakland	White to Black
0.15	Perry South	White to Black
0.17	Lincoln	White to Black
0.25	Manchester	White to Black
0.26	Garfield-Bloomfield	White to Black
0.47	Point Breeze	White to Black
0.59	Garfield	White to Black
0.10	Shadyside	White to Nonsegregated

Racial change was found to have occurred in all six possible directions (black to white, black to nonsegregated, white to black, white to nonsegregated, nonsegregated to black, and nonsegregated to white) over the forty-year period. (The tracts that experienced racial change are listed in Appendix B with their

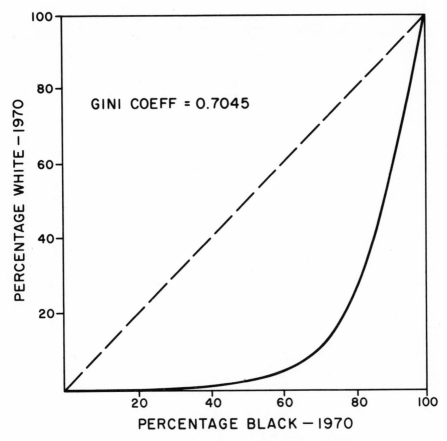

Figure 2-9. Residential Segregation of Afro-Americans in Pittsburgh, 1970

racial deficits, population numbers, and tract percentage black.) In each decade, however, racial change occurred only in census tracts whose percent racial deficits in the preceding decade were less than one percent. This may indicate an upper limit to the amount of racial change practical or possible under the circumstances prevailing in 1930-1970.

Notes

1. See Otis Dudley Duncan, and Beverly Duncan, THE NEGRO POPU-LATION OF CHICAGO: A STUDY OF RESIDENTIAL SUCCESSION (Chicago: University of Chicago Press, 1957), pp. 11 and 12; also Alma F. Taeuber,

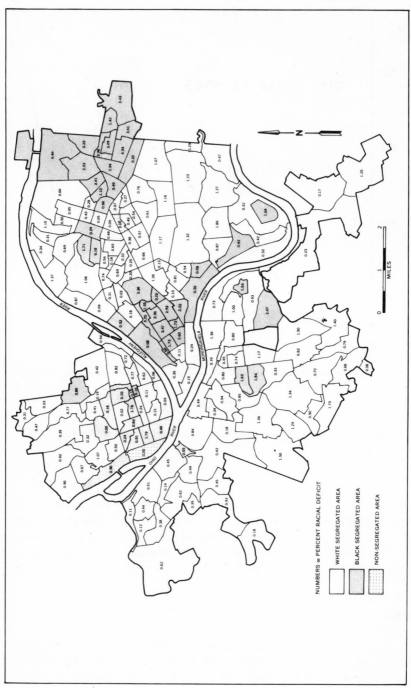

Figure 2-10. Spatial Pattern of Afro-American Residential Segregation in Pittsburgh, 1970

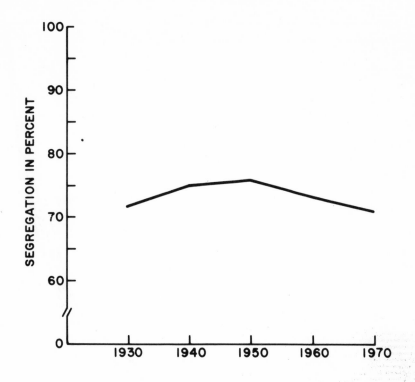

Figure 2-11. Trends in Afro-American Residential Segregation in Pittsburgh, 1930-1970

"Comparative Urban Analysis of Negro Residential Succession" (unpublished Ph.D. dissertation, University of Chicago, 1962), chapter 2; and Karl E. Taeuber and Alma F. Taeuber, NEGROES IN CITIES: RESIDENTIAL SEGREGATION AND NEIGHBORHOOD CHANGE (Chicago: Aldine Publishing Co., 1965), pp. 105-14.

2. See Duncan and Duncan, THE NEGRO POPULATION OF CHICAGO, pp. 142-56, and Taeuber and Taeuber, NEGROES IN CITIES, pp. 166-73.

3. Room crowding can be quantitatively defined as the percentage of households consisting of 2 or more persons living in dwelling units with 1.51 or more persons per room.

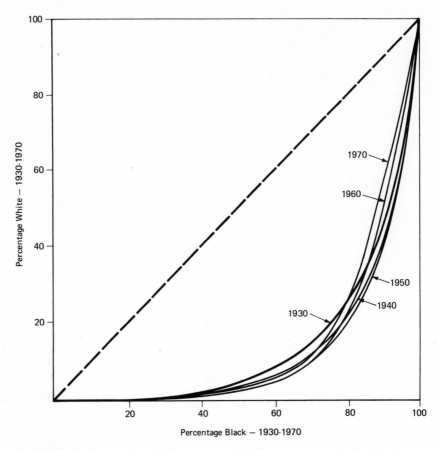

Figure 2-12. Residential Segregation of Afro-Americans in Pittsburgh, 1930-1970

3 Housing Cost as a Factor in Racial Residential Segregation

The preceding chapter showed that residential segregation of Afro-Americans in Pittsburgh remained at a high level from 1930 to 1970. This chapter and the next will examine the relative effects of housing cost inequality and racial discrimination on Pittsburgh's residential segregation. The purpose of this chapter is to determine how much residential segregation can be explained by housing cost inequality. The time period covered is 1940-1970, since data on economic factors by race and census tract were not available prior to 1940.

A Preliminary Measure

Given the fact that blacks have a lower average economic status than whites, let us assume that most black homeowners live in low-value housing and most black renters in low-rent housing, while most whites live in high-value or high-rent housing. Does this assumption allow us to conclude that the high level of segregation between blacks and whites is merely a function of segregation between low-value and high-value housing or low-rent and high-rent housing? If so, a Gini index of segregation between blacks and whites should be approximately equal to a Gini index of segregation between low-value and high-value housing and low-rent and high-rent housing.

As a preliminary exploration of the effects of housing cost (prior to the major analysis presented later in this chapter), such a comparison was made. "High value" was defined as housing value above the median for the city as a whole, and "high rent" as rent above the median for the city as a whole.[1]

In 1940 the amount of segregation (Gini index) between low-value and high-value housing regardless of race was 40.7 percent (Figure 3-1). If all the black homeowners of Pittsburgh had lived in low-value housing and all the white homeowners in high value housing, the amount of segregation between the two groups would also have been 40.7 percent.

The distribution of low-rent and high-rent housing in 1940 shows less segregation, only 33.9 percent (Figure 3-2). If all black renters of Pittsburgh had lived in low-rent housing and all white renters in high-rent housing, the amount of segregation between the two groups would have been 33.9 percent.

Thus, the mean index of segregation for all housing in Pittsburgh in 1940 was $\frac{(40.7 + 33.9)}{2}$, or 37.3 percent. This was 37.6 percentage points lower than Pittsburgh's racial residential segregation index (74.9 percent) for that year.

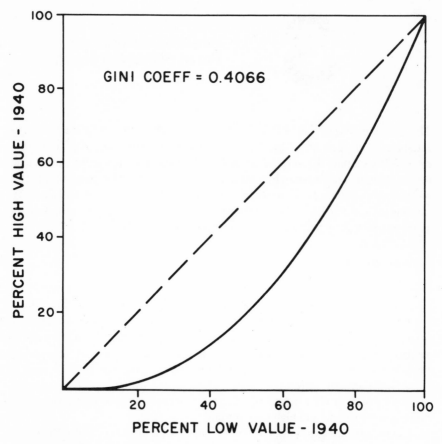

Figure 3-1. The Spatial Segregation of Low-Value and High-Value Housing in Pittsburgh, 1940

By 1950, the amount of spatial segregation between low-value and high-value housing had decreased by 3.7 percentage points to 37.0 percent (Figure 3-3). The segregation between low-rent and high-rent housing was 35.4 percent (Figure 3-4), an increase of 1.5 percentage points. Thus the mean index of segregation for all housing in 1950 was $\frac{(37.0 + 35.4)}{2}$, or 36.2 percent, which was 39.5 percentage points lower than the index for segregation between blacks and whites (75.7 percent).

Segregation between low-value and high-value housing reached an all-time low in 1960, when it amounted to 33.4 percent (Figure 3-5), a decrease of 3.6 percentage points from 1950. On the other hand, the level of segregation

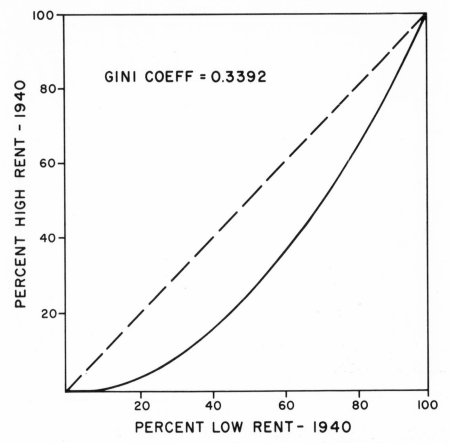

Figure 3-2. The Spatial Segregation of Low-Rent and High-Rent Housing in Pittsburgh, 1940

between low-rent and high-rent housing continued to increase, from 35.4 percent in 1950 to 36.2 percent in 1960 (Figure 3-6). Thus the mean index of segregation for all housing in 1960 was $\frac{(33.4 + 36.2)}{2}$, or 34.8 percent, which was 38.1 percentage points lower than the index for segregation between blacks and whites (72.9 percent).

The level of segregation between low-value and high-value housing rose during the 1960s, reaching 40.9 percent in 1970 (Figure 3-7). This was the highest level of segregation between low-value and high-value housing reached during the study period. The level of segregation between low-rent and high-rent housing also reached its maximum in 1970, at 37.8 percent (Figure 3-8). Thus the mean

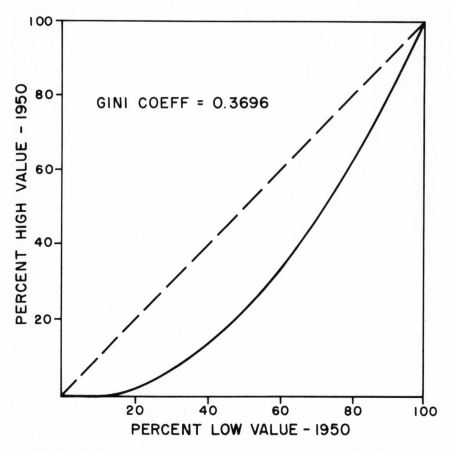

Figure 3-3. The Spatial Segregation of Low-Value and High-Value Housing in Pittsburgh, 1950

index of segregation for all housing in 1970 was $\dfrac{(40.9 + 37.8)}{2}$, or 39.3 percent, which was 31.2 percentage points lower than the index for segregation between blacks and whites (70.5).

In summary, as Table 3-1 shows, from 1940 to 1970, the level of segregation between low-value and high-value housing and between low-rent and high-rent housing remained 31.2 to 39.5 percentage points lower than the level of segregation between blacks and whites. Thus, if all blacks in Pittsburgh had lived in low-value or low-rent housing and all whites in high-value or high-rent housing from 1940 to 1970, the amount of segregation between blacks and whites would have been from 31.2 to 39.5 percentage points less than it actually was.

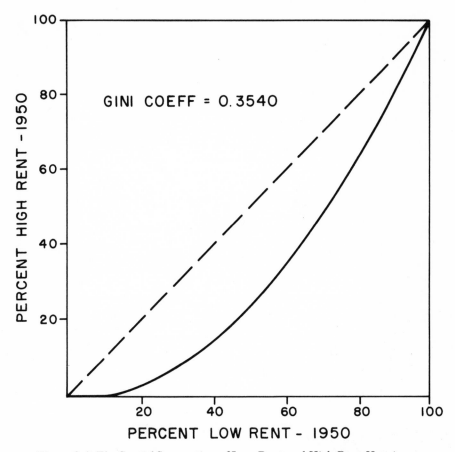

Figure 3-4. The Spatial Segregation of Low-Rent and High-Rent Housing in Pittsburgh, 1950

Though this does not give us a precise measure of the effect of spatial segregation of housing on racial residential segregation, it does make one thing clear. If racial residential segregation in Pittsburgh were solely due to segregation of housing in terms of value and rent, then racial residential segregation could not have been higher than 34.8 to 39.3 percent from 1940 to 1970. Therefore we cannot conclude that the observed high level (70.5 to 75.7) of racial residential segregation was merely a function of segregation between low-value and high-value housing and between low-rent and high-rent housing. To determine how much racial residential segregation can be explained by housing cost inequality, we turn to correlation and regression analysis, as described below.

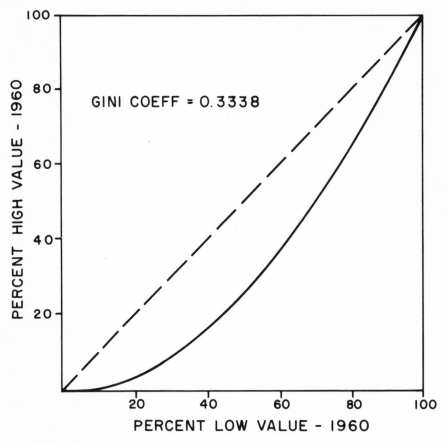

Figure 3-5. The Spatial Segregation of Low-Value and High-Value Housing in Pittsburgh, 1960

A More Precise Measure

To ascertain the relative significance of housing cost in explaining racial residential segregation, the four economic variables low rent, high rent, low value, and high value were regressed against percent black in a stepwise regression model.[2] Stepwise regression involves the computation of successive regression analyses. The computer is programmed to select from the independent variables (in this case, the four economic variables) the one that is "best," i.e., that has the highest partial correlation with the dependent variable (in this case, percent black by census tract).[3] It then selects additional variables in the order of the amount of their additional contribution. Since the four independent

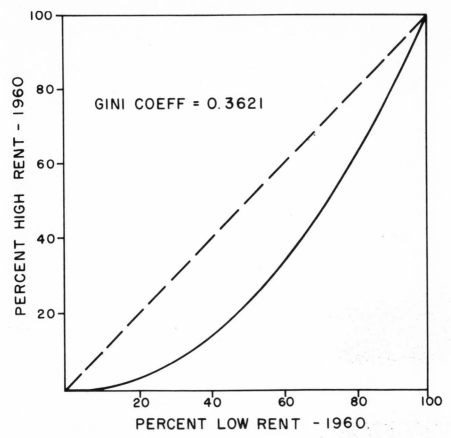

GINI COEFF = 0.3621

Figure 3-6. The Spatial Segregation of Low-Rent and High-Rent Housing in Pittsburgh, 1960

variables are highly intercorrelated, together they are considered the "housing cost factor."

Stepwise regression analysis was carried out for the decades 1940-1970, and the results are presented in Tables 3-2 to 3-5. In these tables, the coefficient of multiple correlation, R, indicates the total strength of the relationship between the dependent and the independent variables. The coefficient of determination, R^2, provides an estimate of the proportion of the total spatial variation in the dependent variable that can be explained by the independent variables. The tables are cumulative, so that the second line shows results for the first two variables combined, the third for the first three, and the fourth for all four together.

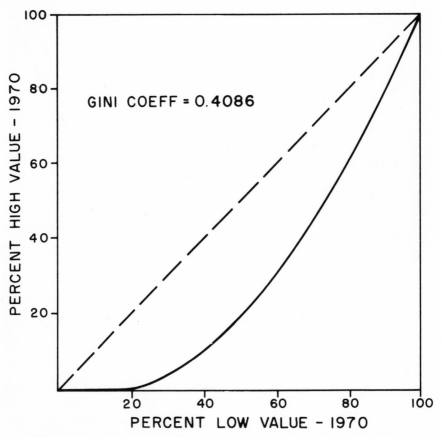

Figure 3-7. The Spatial Segregation of Low-Value and High-Value Housing in Pittsburgh, 1970

In 1940, low rent was the most important economic variable in explaining racial residential segregation (Table 3-2). This variable was followed by high value, low value, and high rent. Together, the four variables explained only 7 percent of the total spatial variation in the dependent variable, leaving 93 percent of the variation still unexplained.

In 1950, high value was the most important economic variable in explaining racial residential segregation (Table 3-3). It was followed by low value, high rent, and low rent. Together, the variables explained 18 percent of the total variation. Clearly, more racial residential segregation could be attributed to housing cost inequality in 1950 than in 1940. However, in 1950 as in 1940, a very large portion of the total variation (82 percent) remained unexplained.

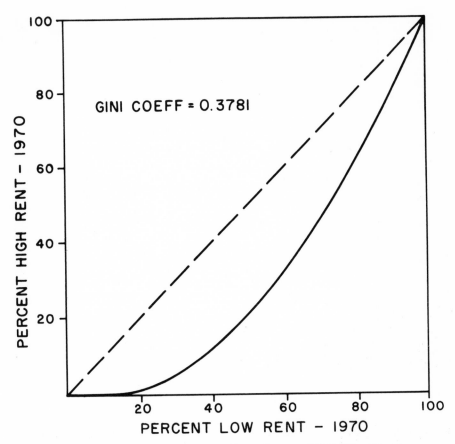

Figure 3-8. The Spatial Segregation of Low-Rent and High-Rent Housing in Pittsburgh, 1970

In 1960, low value was the most significant economic variable in explaining racial residential segregation (Table 3-4). The succeeding variables were high value, high rent, and low rent. These variables explained 16 percent of the total variation, showing that less segregation could be attributed to the housing cost factor in 1960 than in 1950. As in prior years, most (84 percent in 1960) of the total variation remained unexplained.

In 1970, the most important economic variable in explaining residential segregation was low value. It was followed by high value, low rent, and high rent (Table 3-5). Together, the variables explained only 15 percent of the total variation in the dependent variable, leaving 85 percent unexplained.

Thus, the housing cost factor may explain from 7 percent to 18 percent of

Table 3-1

Indexes of Segregation on the Basis of Race, Housing Value, and Rent, 1940-1970

Year	Race	Housing Value	Rent
1940	74.9%	40.7%	33.9%
1950	75.7%	37.0%	35.4%
1960	72.9%	33.4%	36.2%
1970	70.5%	40.9%	37.8%

Table 3-2

Coefficients of Multiple Correlation, Multiple Determination, and Unexplained Variation: Stepwise Regression Analysis, 1940

Variable	R	R^2	Unexplained Variation
Percent Low Rent	.25	6%	94%
Percent High Value	.27	7%	93%
Percent Low Value	.27	7%	93%
Percent High Rent	.27	7%	93%

Table 3-3

Coefficients of Multiple Correlation, Multiple Determination, and Unexplained Variation: Stepwise Regression Analysis, 1950

Variable	R	R^2	Unexplained Variation
Percent High Value	.41	17%	83%
Percent Low Value	.42	17%	83%
Percent High Rent	.42	17%	83%
Percent Low Rent	.43	18%	82%

Table 3-4

Coefficients of Multiple Correlation, Multiple Determination, and Unexplained Variation: Stepwise Regression Analysis, 1960

Variable	R	R^2	Unexplained Variation
Percent Low Value	.39	15%	85%
Percent High Value	.40	16%	84%
Percent High Rent	.40	16%	84%
Percent Low Rent	.40	16%	84%

Table 3-5
Coefficients of Multiple Correlation, Multiple Determination, and Unexplained Variation: Stepwise Regression Analysis, 1970

Variable	R	R^2	Unexplained Variation
Percent Low Value	.37	13%	87%
Percent High Value	.38	14%	86%
Percent Low Rent	.39	15%	85%
Percent High Rent	.39	15%	85%

the residential segregation in Pittsburgh during the study period. For an explanation of by far the greater part of the segregation in Pittsburgh, we must look elsewhere.

Summary and Conclusions

This chapter has examined the influence of housing cost on racial residential segregation in Pittsburgh from 1940 to 1970. As a means of preliminary exploration, Gini indices were calculated showing the segregation of low-value from high-value housing and of low-rent from high-rent housing for each decade, and these were compared with the Gini index for racial residential segregation. The results showed that segregation on the basis of housing value and segregation on the basis of rent were much lower than segregation on the basis of race. If the segregation of the black population were solely due to segregation between low-value housing and high-value housing for homeowners and between low-rent and high-rent housing for those who rent, the maximum possible level of racial segregation would have been far below the level actually observed. Thus, some segregation must have another explanation.

Correlation and regression analysis then demonstrated that from 1940 to 1970, only 7 percent to 18 percent of the segregation that existed could be explained by housing cost (Table 3-6). Clearly, this analysis confirms the hypothesis that the high level of residential segregation in Pittsburgh has not been caused by housing cost inequality.

Notes

1. For the purpose of this study, "value" is defined as the amount for which the owner estimates that the property, including any land that belongs with it, would sell if it were for sale. The value data are limited to owner-occupied one-family houses on less than ten acres, without a commercial establishment or

Table 3-6
Summary of Multiple Determination and Unexplained Variation, 1940-1970

Year	R^2	Unexplained Variation
1940	7%	93%
1950	18%	82%
1960	16%	84%
1970	15%	85%

medical office on the property. Owner-occupied cooperatives, condominiums, mobile homes, and trailers are excluded from the value tabulations. "Rent" in this study refers to contract monthly rent for the years 1940, 1950, and 1970 and gross monthly rent for 1960. Data on the distribution of contract monthly rent for 1960 were not available. Contract rent is monthly rent agreed to, or contracted for, even if the furnishings, utilities, or services are included. Gross rent on the other hand is the contract rent plus the average monthly cost of utilities. For the years 1940, 1950, 1960, and 1970, Pittsburgh's median housing value was, respectively, $4,267, $8,293, $11,000, and $15,300, and its median rent $24.62, $35.83, $68.00, and $76.00. See U.S., Department of Commerce, Bureau of the Census, SIXTEENTH CENSUS OF THE UNITED STATES, 1940: POPULATION AND HOUSING, Vol. 7, STATISTICS FOR CENSUS TRACTS, Pittsburgh; U.S., Department of Commerce, Bureau of the Census, UNITED STATES CENSUS OF POPULATION: 1950, Vol. 3, CENSUS TRACT STATIS- TICS, Pittsburgh; also U.S., Department of Commerce, Bureau of the Census, UNITED STATES CENSUS OF POPULATION: 1960, Vol. 1, CHARACTERIS- TICS OF THE POPULATION: CENSUS TRACTS, Pittsburgh; and U.S., Depart- ment of Commerce, Bureau of the Census, UNITED STATES CENSUS OF HOUSING: 1970, Advance Report; GENERAL HOUSING CHARACTERIS- TICS, Pennsylvania.

2. For a discussion of the model used in this study see J.W. Dixon, ed., BIOMEDICAL COMPUTER PROGRAMS (Berkeley: University of California Press, 1968), pp. 215-33.

3. See, N.R. Draper and H. Smith, APPLIED REGRESSION ANALYSIS (New York: John Wiley and Sons, Inc., 1967), pp. 171-72.

4

Racial Discrimination as a Factor in Residential Segregation

... when racial discrimination herds men into ghettos and makes their ability to buy property turn on the color of their skin, then it too is a relic of slavery.

−U.S. Supreme Court[1]

In the preceding chapter it was demonstrated that the housing cost factor accounts for only a minimal amount of the racial residential segregation in Pittsburgh. This chapter deals with racial discrimination in housing in an attempt to determine whether the unexplained segregation of the previous chapter is due to racial discrimination.

For the purpose of this study, racial discrimination in housing refers to any actions which enforce residential restrictions against blacks. Data on discrimination were obtained from the files of the Pittsburgh Commission on Human Relations, the files of the United States District Court for Western Pennyvania, interviews with real estate brokers, and research material relevant to racial discrimination in housing.

This chapter will focus primarily on the period mid-1959-1970. Data are limited prior to that time, since no enforceable legal measures against racial residential discrimination were available in Pittsburgh until June 1, 1959, when the 1958 Fair Housing Ordinance of Pittsburgh became effective. In fact, until 1948, when the United States Supreme Court ruled against the enforcement by courts of racially restrictive convenants on the sale of property,[2] racial discrimination in housing throughout the United States was given legal, social, and economic sanction. The prevailing attitudes of white America were best stated by the United States Federal Housing Administration in 1938 and again in 1947. In 1938 the Administration stated:

Areas surrounding a location are investigated to determine whether incompatible racial and social groups are present, for the purpose of making a prediction regarding the probability of a location being invaded by such groups. If a neighborhood is to retain stability, it is necessary that properties shall continue to be occupied by the same social and racial classes.[3]

In 1947 it stated:

Protective covenants are essential to the sound development of proposed residential areas since they regulate the use of the land and provide a basis for

41

the development of harmonious, attractive neighborhoods suitable and desirable to the user groups forming the potential markets.[4]

The extent of racial discrimination in housing in Pittsburgh is a function of two opposing forces, "discriminating" forces operating to segregate residential areas on the basis of race and "antidiscriminating" forces operating to desegregate them. The discriminatory force with which this study deals consist of white real estate brokers and salesmen, white real estate organizations, white owners of dwellings, white financial institutions, white newspapers, and white home builders. The antidiscriminatory forces are the Pittsburgh Commission on Human Relations, black real estate brokers and salesmen, and black financial institutions.

Impact of Discriminating Forces on the Maintenance and Increase of Residential Segregation

Complaints of Discrimination, 1959-1970

Table 4-1 lists the discriminating forces with the percent of complaints against them from June 1, 1959, to December 31, 1970. The role of each is discussed in the sections which follow. White real estate organizations, also discussed, do not appear on the table because their role in segregation involves the real estate business itself rather than individual black candidates for housing.

Table 4-2 again shows percent of complaints, this time by the type of transaction involved. As the table shows, the great majority of complaints concerned rentals rather than sales, a fact to be expected in a central city. As noted later, this probably affects the relative importance of the discriminatory forces; if suburbs were included in this study, the percentages in both tables would be different.

Table 4-1
Type of Discriminator and Percent of Complaints, 1959-1970

Real Estate Broker or Salesman	51.1
Owner of Dwelling	33.9
Financial Institution	0.6
Newspaper	2.3
Home Builder	0.6
Other	11.5
Total	100.0
	(N=454)

Source: Pittsburgh Commission on Human Relations, 1970 ANNUAL REPORT (Pittsburgh, 1970).

Table 4-2
Type of Transaction and Percent of Complaints, 1959-1970

Apartment Rental	70.7
House Rental	20.2
House Sale	7.2
Lot Sale	1.5
Trailer Space	0.4
Total	100.0
	(N=454)

Source: Pittsburgh Commission on Human Relations, 1970 ANNUAL REPORT (Pittsburgh, 1970).

Table 4-3 shows some of the techniques used by the discriminating forces as reflected in the types of complaint made. Finally, Table 4-4 shows the spatial distribution of the complaints.

With the exception of East Liberty-Larimer (15.6 percent of total complaints), which is a black community, the communities identified in Table 4-4 as having the greatest percentage of complaints are adjacent to sizeable black communities. For example, Oakland-Shadyside (27.9 percent) is very close to the Hill District, one of the largest black communities in Pittsburgh. The Northside (9.6 percent) is on the border of Manchester, a densely populated black community. Squirrel Hill (8.1 percent) is located near Homewood and scattered black communities along the Monongahela River.

Fewer complaints have occurred in communities not adjacent to black communities. This does not necessarily mean that there is less racial discrimination in such communities. It could also mean that fewer blacks have attempted to locate in such communities or, less probably, that fewer blacks who were denied access to such communities filed a complaint. Other things being equal, the percentage of complaints of racial discrimination in any community is a function of the percentage of blacks attempting to locate in such community. Thus, if fewer blacks attempt to locate in white communities not adjacent to black communities, then one can expect fewer complaints. If the small proportion of complaints in these communities were due to less racial discrimination, then one should expect a higher percentage of the black population in those communities. Examination of the census data shows that this has not been the case. The percentage black in tracts located in communities with a high percentage of complaints is at least equal to the percentage black in communities with a low percentage of complaints.

White Real Estate Brokers and White Salesmen

On the basis of percent of complaints, white real estate brokers or salesmen[5] are the most influential of the discriminating forces (Table 4-1). Of the total

Table 4-3

Type of Alleged Violation and Percent of Complaints, 1959-1970

Failure to Process Application	30.4
Refusal to Accept Application	48.9
Cancellation of Lease	9.0
Refusal to Sell Property	5.2
Discriminatory Advertising	2.6
Refusal of Mortgage	0.2
Separate Rental Lists	0.2
Harassment of Seller	0.2
Other	3.3
Total	100.0
	(N=454)

Source: Pittsburgh Commission on Human Relations, 1970 ANNUAL REPORT (Pittsburgh, 1970).

Table 4-4

Spatial Variation of Complaints of Racial Discrimination in Housing by Community, 1959-1970

Community	Percent of Complaints
Downtown (CBD)	0.4
Oakland-Shadyside	27.9
Point Breeze	5.7
Stanton Heights	1.9
East Liberty-Larimer	15.6
Homewood-Brushton	5.9
Squirrel Hill	8.1
Hazelwood-Greenfield	3.9
Hill District	1.9
Herron Hill	0.4
Lawrenceville	2.2
Garfield-Bloomfield	3.7
Northside	9.6
Brookline-Beechview-Banksville	1.3
Southside	1.9
Mt. Washington-Knoxville	1.3
West End-Sheraden-Elliott	2.6
Other Areas of the City	5.7
Total	100.0
	(N=454)

Source: Pittsburgh Commission on Human Relations, 1970 ANNUAL REPORT (Pittsburgh, 1970).

complaints recorded in the period studied (numbering 454), 51.1 percent were against this group. White brokers and salesmen play a key role in perpetuating residential segregation. They have been operating within a segregated system and for a segregated city since the beginning of their business operations, many of which date back before 1930. Therefore they have a head start on the antidiscriminating forces, which have been operating effectively only since 1960.

The discriminatory behavior and attitudes of the white brokers of Pittsburgh have been confirmed by 1965 and 1967 surveys by the Pittsburgh Commission on Human Relations. The 1965 survey revealed that a majority of the responding brokers had never shown Negro prospects housing for sale in segregated white communities prior to 1965. Approximately three-fourths had never shown rental housing nor completed a sale or rental in such circumstances. Moreover the majority of brokers disapproved of or actively opposed Fair Housing laws in 1965 because of their belief that their owner clients were opposed to Fair Housing laws.[6]

The 1967 survey showed that 62 percent of the responding brokers had shown black clients housing for sale in a segregated white community at least one or more times, though only 15 percent had done so more than 10 times. Approximately two-fifths of the sample group had completed a sale in such a situation. Only 45 percent of the responding brokers had shown rental housing to black prospects in a white community, and only a third of the sample group had actually rented to black tenants in such a community.[7]

Fifty-two percent of the brokers responding in 1967 indicated that they favored a nondiscriminatory housing market, in which prospective buyers and tenants are not restricted in their choice on the basis of race, religion, or national origin. On the other hand, 31 percent, a substantial minority, indicated opposition to such a housing market. These results show a slight increase (up from 48 percent in 1965) in the proportion in favor and a modest decrease (down from 36 percent) in the proportion opposed. While a majority of the brokers indicated that they themselves favored a nondiscriminatory housing market, an even larger majority—66 percent—believed that most of their clients opposed a nondiscriminatory market. Only 17 percent believed that a majority of their clients were in favor of such a housing market.[8] It appears that the real estate brokers were justifying their discriminatory behavior and attitudes by claiming that they were merely following the instructions of their clients. However, it is brokers themselves who are usually the instructors. People ask for and follow the broker's advice when buying, selling, renting, altering, insuring, trading, and appraising property. They are the ones who can change land use, standards of occupancy, and the racial and ethnic pattern of occupancy in an area.[9]

In a study published in 1966 of 45 black families who had moved into seven segregated white wards in Pittsburgh,[10] slightly under a third of the families indicated that they had encountered problems in looking for and obtaining housing. Problems due to race were cited more often than any other; 29 percent of the families said they had had problems either looking for or obtaining their homes because of their race. The difficulty was evidently not housing cost since almost all (93 percent) of those who had encountered problems were in the upper income or upper middle income group. Seventy-seven percent of the families citing racial problems resided in high-income areas.[11]

Thirty-one percent of the racial problems mentioned involved discriminatory practices on the part of real estate brokers and landlords. Several of the black families expressed the view that it is the real estate brokers who are responsible for continuing segregation.

More evidence that race is the major explanatory factor in residential segregation is provided by the public hearings of the Pittsburgh Commission on Human Relations regarding four cases of racial discrimination from 1959 to 1965. All four cases involved Negroes of substantial economic standing. All were professionals—two being physicians, one engineer with a national corporation, and one professional social worker. Each was highly respected among his colleagues and was a leader in local community projects. Finally, each had a desire to secure safe, decent, and sanitary housing in a setting of his choice but was rebuffed in this effort.[12]

As one searches for a logical rationale for the brokers' discriminatory behavior, one turns to economics. White real estate brokers realize an economic gain in excluding blacks from the white communities of Pittsburgh. Such exclusion leads to overcrowding and a limited supply of housing for blacks, thus forcing blacks to pay higher prices for the housing that is available. White residents of Pittsburgh have benefited as well because the exclusion of blacks from white residential areas reduces the competition for housing in white areas, lowering housing and rental costs. According to Helper's analysis of Chicago, brokers are of the opinion that property, once transferred from white to Negro hands, is lost to the white groups forever. Hence, prospects for future gain by that property and all possibilities for future white control by ownership of the land and property are lost. The conclusion was based on the view that Negroes resell property less often than do white people and that the white people seldom buy and live in property that has been occupied by Negroes. Helper then states that when such property is sold to blacks the broker in charge is usually Negro.[13]

Though the primary beneficiaries of racial discrimination thus appear to be the white brokers, they continue in their efforts to persuade the public that the decision to discriminate is made not by them but by the property owners. The National Association of Real Estate Boards in its "1965 Statement of Policy" emphasized that, "No realtor should assume to determine the suitability or eligibility on racial, creedal, or ethnic grounds of any prospective mortgagor, tenant, or purchaser."[14] In the same statement they emphasized the freedom of the property owners to "determine the suitability or eligibility of any prospective mortgagor, tenant, or purchaser on racial, creedal, or ethnic grounds."[15]

In summary, the most influential element among the discriminating forces seems to be the white real estate broker or salesman,[16] presumably because of the economic benefits of segregation to this group. The end result has been the exclusion of blacks from white residential communities of Pittsburgh.

White Real Estate Organizations

An effective discriminatory technique used by the white real estate business has been to exclude black real estate brokers and black salesmen from membership in its organizations. Two major real estate organizations in Pittsburgh of significance to black brokers and salesmen are the Greater Pittsburgh Board of Realtors and the Greater Pittsburgh Multilist, Inc. (formerly called East-End Multilist, Inc.). Of the two, Multilist is probably the most important for economic or business purposes and in terms of influencing residential segregation. Of the eleven black real estate brokers in Pittsburgh, only four are members of the Greater Pittsburgh Board of Realtors and only two are members of the Greater Pittsburgh Multilist, Inc.[17] prior to 1967, all of the officers and members of Multilist were white, and it was therefore extremely difficult for the first black broker to acquire membership. Only after a court order was the first black broker, Robert Lavelle, admitted.[18] Lavelle requested membership on May 12, 1965. On May 25, 1965, he received a letter from the Chairman of the Multilist Membership Committee stating that the procedure for applying for membership requires that he obtain two sponsors. It took two months to obtain the required sponsors. Robert Lavelle submitted his completed application and a check for the $500 membership fee on September 2, 1965. On September 23, Lavelle was informed by letter that Multilist did not approve his application for membership. The check was returned. On September 27, Lavelle wrote to Multilist noting that he had not been given a reason for the rejection of his application and requested reconsideration and an opportunity to appear before the membership and answer any questions the membership might have. On September 30, Multilist responded that "the one and only reason [for rejection] was that your office simply did not receive the required three-fourths affirmative vote for acceptance" and that the matter was "conclusively closed." On February 24, 1966, Lavelle wrote individually to the thirty-three members of Multilist requesting opportunities to meet at their individual convenience and discuss any problems they might have concerning his application. He received eight responses and six interviews. One white real estate broker expressed his concern that Lavelle would "agitate." On October 5, 1966, Lavelle submitted his second application for membership, together with the required fee and letters of sponsorship. On December 5, he received a letter from Multilist's Membership Chairman informing him that his application was rejected. Again, no reason was stated other than, "the written ballot results were that it was rejected."

Meanwhile, Multilist had admitted white brokers to membership during and after the period in which Lavelle was rejected. Did Lavelle satisfy all of the requirements for membership?

Multilist By-Laws state five qualifications for membership: (1) Pennsylvania real estate broker's license; (2) Class A membership in a board of realtors affiliated with the National Association of Real Estate Boards; (3) good character and good reputation; (4) negotiation and consummation of twelve real estate sales in the twelve months preceding the application; and (5) conduct of business for at least two years in the Multilist territory. Additionally, a rejected applicant may not reapply for a six-month period following rejection of his application.[19] On each item, Lavelle qualified. Therefore, according to Judge Marsh, the presiding judge in the District Court of Western Pennsylvania, the exclusion of Lavelle from membership was due to a conspiracy[20] of white members of Multilist to exclude black brokers from membership.[21]

The Greater Pittsburgh Multilist, Inc., until recently known as the Greater East-End Multilist, Inc., is a nonprofit membership corporation organized under the laws of Pennsylvania.[22] It is an affiliate of the Greater Pittsburgh Board of Realtors and the National Association of Real Estate Boards (NAREB). The main purpose of Multilist is to consolidate and distribute to each of its members all the real property listings of other members.[23] The organization's membership territory includes Pittsburgh's central business district on the west and is bound on the south by the Monongahela River, on the north by the Allegheny River, and on the east by the city line.[24] It includes over one-half of both the land and the population of the city of Pittsburgh.

In the conduct of their business, the members of the Greater Pittsburgh Multilist represent owners and lessors of real property transferred within their jurisdiction. Within four days of acceptance, every member of Multilist must supply a copy of every exclusive listing contract he secures, together with a photograph; these are then distributed to all members of the organization. Listing brokers retain exclusive rights for seven days. Multilist regulates the activities of listing office and selling offices. Three percent of the gross commission is paid to the corporation (Multilist); of the balance, 70 percent is then kept by the selling office and 30 percent is paid to the listing office. In 1967, more than thirty-five brokers were members of Multilist. Robert Lavelle and other black brokers or salesmen had lost, and were continuing to lose, considerable sales opportunities because they were barred from showing potential and long-term customers properties listed through this organization.

During the first eleven months of 1967, Multilist listed approximately 830 properties, with a combined value of more than $17 million.[25] During this same period, approximately 460 properties were sold through Multilist, with a total value exceeding $8.65 million. During 1966, over 900 properties were listed, with a total value of approximately $19.78 million, and approximately 440 properties were sold for a total value of approximately $8.2 million. From the creation of Greater Pittsburgh Multilist in 1958 to 1967, nearly 10,000 properties were listed, with a total value of approximately $200 million.

At least two million dollars of mortgages on Multilist sales were obtained during 1967 from mortgagees located outside the State of Pennsylvania. These mortgages were financed by banks and savings and loan associations which are substantially engaged in interstate commerce. Insurance was secured from insurance companies which were substantially engaged in interstate commerce and many of which were located in states other than Pennsylvania. Therefore, in the opinion of Judge Marsh, the white brokers of Greater Pittsburgh Multilist were engaged in an unlawful combination and conspiracy in the restriction of the interstate trade and commerce. Thus, they were in violation of Section One of the Sherman Act.[26]

The objectives of this conspiracy were to exclude black brokers from membership in Greater Pittsburgh Multilist, to prevent black persons from owning and renting real property located in neighborhoods of Pittsburgh occupied solely or primarily by white persons, and to limit membership in Multilist, with its benefits, thereby avoiding a reduction in the business and income of white brokers.[27] Its consequences were far-reaching. They were as follows: (1) interstate commerce in building materials and supplies was substantially affected and restrained because black real estate brokers and salesmen who ordinarily would procure customers for such building materials and supplies were barred from doing so; (2) interstate commerce in mortgage financing and insurance was similarly affected and restrained because black real estate brokers and salesmen who would ordinarily procure customers were barred from doing so; (3) substantial numbers of black persons from outside Pennsylvania were probably prevented from entering Pittsburgh because their opportunities to buy or rent property there were limited; (4) black brokers and salesmen were unable to service customers wanting to buy or rent real property located in the white segregated areas of Pittsburgh; (5) white owners and renters of real property were deprived of the opportunity to deal with black brokers and black salesmen and their customers; (6) black brokers suffered a substantial loss of income as a result of being deprived of access to the listings shared by members of Greater Pittsburgh Multilist; and (7) black persons have been limited to housing facilities in black segregated areas of Pittsburgh.

To summarize, the evidence indicates that the white real estate members of Greater Pittsburgh Multilist, the dominant multiple listing organization in the city, had been conspiring to exclude black brokers from membership from its creation in 1958 to 1967.[28] Their motive appears to have been economic gain at the expense of the black brokers and black home seekers. The ultimate results were the limitation of blacks to certain residential areas of the city of Pittsburgh, and thus the maintenance of residential segregation on the basis of race.

White Owners

White owners of dwellings are second to white brokers as a force of discrimination. Of the 454 complaints made from June 1, 1959, to December 31, 1970,

33.9 percent involved white owners (Table 4-1). In most of these cases, blacks attempted to rent an apartment and were refused by the landlord.[29] The motive for their discriminatory behavior cannot be readily established. Perhaps it is outright racism,[30] or else the belief that if they rent to a black person, white tenants may vacate the building, thereby resulting in an economic loss, at least temporarily. Whatever the reason, the effect is the same. This discriminatory action denies blacks access to many areas of the city of Pittsburgh. Thus, residential segregation increases or is maintained at a high level.

White Financial Institutions

White financial institutions have the power to influence the residential locations of many black homeowners in the United States.[31] However, in Pittsburgh, there is little evidence to support any claim that they have done so. Of the total complaints from June 1, 1959, to December 31, 1970, only 0.6 percent involved financial institutions (Table 4-1). Further evidence that their role as a discriminatory force has been minor appears in a recent study, in which the respondents indicated that problems in obtaining credit or mortgages in Pittsburgh did not appear to them to involve racial injustices.[32] Another survey, including but not limited to Pittsburgh, showed that restrictions on financing of Negro purchases in previously white areas have disappeared or diminished. The study, based on 1960 data, further stated that "a number of leading institutional investors are now on record as willing to extend credit to any qualified person in any area." Most have dropped the line for race of applicant from their mortgage application forms.[33]

To summarize, on the basis of the scanty data available, there is little evidence to support an accusation of widespread discrimination by white financial institutions in recent years. But residential segregation is an accumulative process that evolves over time, and the past role of white financial institutions cannot be adequately estimated or investigated. Their relatively minor role as a discriminating force in recent years could be attributed to the fact that they are always the second link in the chain of operation. In other words, a black home seeker must have preselected the home and area of location prior to applying for a mortgage loan. If the location is in a segregated white community, the process of exclusion or denial is usually carried out by the first link in the chain, that is, the white broker or white owner. This reduces the number of times the mortgage lending institution has an opportunity to take discriminatory action. In addition, financial institutions only deal with potential black purchasers, not renters. Thus, at least half of the black population does not come in contact with financial institutions, further reducing the percent of complaints of discrimination against this force.

White Newspapers

As in the case of white financial institutions, the percent of complaints against white newspapers has been relatively small. From June 1, 1959, to December 31, 1970, only 2.3 percent of the total complaints were filed against white newspapers for discriminatory advertising (Table 4-1). One must not assume, however, that complaints alone can adequately measure the impact of this discriminatory force on residential segregation. The actual influence of discriminatory advertising on the behavior of blacks and the choice of living space is probably far greater. To determine the extent of this effect would require a survey in itself and is beyond the scope of the present study, but further investigation in this area is greatly needed.

Discriminatory advertisements have changed their form over the years as a result of antidiscriminatory forces, but their effect probably remains. The following discriminating advertisements are typical of those regularly carried by newspapers prior to 1960:

Homewood—Colored: 3 rooms, bath, apt. bldg. $62.50 Ch-2-3200[34]

Homes for Colored—Reasonable Good Location—Terms Jacob L. Phillips, Broker 6286—Broad Street MO-1-2061[35]

After 1960, advertisements changed their form. Several discriminatory euphemisms emerged, of which the most commonly used are "restricted" and "exclusive." The advertisement below is typical.

Lots for Sale
Chartiers County Club—Haddock
View Acres. Restricted Lot
276-5677[36]

The advertisement above has a dual purpose. It immediately assuages the fears of racially prejudiced whites and informs blacks that they should not apply, or if they should apply, they can expect to encounter discrimination.

To summarize, white newspapers as a discriminating force have left their stamp on residential segregation. The magnitude of their influence awaits further research.

White Home Builders

The role of white home builders as a discriminatory force in the city of Pittsburgh has been minor in comparison to other forces. From June 1, 1959, to December 31, 1970, only 0.6 percent of the total complaints were filed against home builders. This small percent of complaints however, should not be misinterpreted. Most of the complaints in Pittsburgh have involved apartment or house rental (Table 4-2). Also, Pittsburgh, like most large central cities, is a highly built-up area. Few people, white or black, are building homes in the central city. If the study had covered the entire Pittsburgh Standard Metropolitan Statistical Area, the percent of complaints against white home builders might have been higher.

Impact of Antidiscriminating Forces on the Decrease in Residential Segregation

Pittsburgh Commission on Human Relations

Although the Pittsburgh Commission on Human Relations was established in June of 1955, its powers were only investigatory until June of 1959,[37] when the first Fair Housing Law of Pittsburgh became effective.[38] Pittsburgh was the second city in the nation (after New York) to pass a fair housing law. The purpose of the law was to prevent and eliminate practices of discrimination in rental, sale, purchase, or financing of residential housing because of race, color, religion, ancestry, or national origin. The law forbids the following acts:

1. To deny an equal opportunity to purchase, sell, lease, sublease, rent, assign or otherwise transfer or refuse to negotiate on any of these matters or to represent that such property is not available for inspection when it is so available.
2. To discriminate in the terms, conditions or privileges in the use or occupancy of a housing unit.
3. To discriminate in the furnishing of any facilities or services of a housing unit.
4. To deny financing, mortgage, loan guarantee or other funds for purchase, construction, rehabilitation, repair or maintenance of any housing unit or housing accommodation.
5. To publish or circulate any notice, statement or advertisement or to announce a policy, or to use any form of application, or to make any record or inquiry which specifies any limitation or discrimination.
6. To obstruct or prevent enforcement or compliance with this ordinance.[39]

A complaint may be filed against any of the following: (1) any real estate broker, salesman, or agent; (2) any owner of five or more dwelling units; (3) any lending institution; and (4) any other person who participates in obstructing or preventing enforcement or compliance with the ordinance.

It is the responsibility of the commission to enforce the law according to established procedure. The receipt of a complaint is immediately followed by a series of confidential discussions with the complainant and the alleged discriminator for the purpose of conciliation.

The failure to resolve a case through private discussions necessitates formal Commission action involving a public hearing and the consequent subpoenaing of witnesses and records. If the commission fails to resolve the case through public hearings, the case is referred to a city magistrate.[40]

A basic weakness in the 1958 ordinance was that it did not apply to owners of fewer than five housing units. In other words, discrimination based on race, religion, nationality, or place of birth was not illegal if an owner owned fewer than five housing units. In recognition of this weakness, a new law was enacted in February of 1967.[41] The new ordinance covers all housing located within the political boundaries of the city of Pittsburgh. The Commission believed that this change gave Pittsburgh the "strongest fair housing ordinance of any city in the nation, with the most complete coverage."[42]

But how strong is the ordinance? The strength of a law rests largely upon the penalty it conveys. The more severe the penalty, the stronger the law. Likewise, the stronger the penalty, the higher the value a community's legislators (Pittsburgh) can be assumed to place upon the seriousness of a crime. Given these assumptions, the ordinance of 1958 was extremely weak and so is the ordinance of 1967. The former ordinance provided for a penalty of $100 or 30 days imprisonment for failure to pay. The latter ordinance provides for a penalty of $300 or 90 days imprisonment for failure to pay. Obviously, Pittsburgh attributes little seriousness to the crime of racial discrimination in housing. Given the small penalty for violation, the average broker or owner would probably prefer to risk the possibility of conviction and conduct discriminatory "business as usual." As previously stated, the most convincing motive for discrimination in housing is economic benefit. Therefore, to be effective, the antidiscriminatory forces must be equipped with the power to deny that benefit. It is likely that once the economic losses as a result of racial discrimination exceed the economic gains, discrimination will cease.

In summary, the Pittsburgh Commission on Human Relations, equipped with the Pittsburgh Fair Housing Ordinance of 1967, is an extremely weak opponent to the forces of discrimination.[43] Thus the primary reasons for the slight decline in residential segregation from 1950 to 1960 and 1960 to 1970 will have to be sought elsewhere.

Black Real Estate Brokers

The impact of the black brokers as an antidiscriminating force was felt only lightly prior to 1967. They merely provided a channel for blacks to move from a more segregated black area to a less segregated black area, as illustrated in Figure 4-1. Typical were movements from the Hill District to Homewood, Beltzhoover, or Manchester. Their power as an antidiscriminating force was severely limited because they were excluded from the white real estate organizations (e.g. Multilist), where listings of properties in all areas of the city were shared. With their recent entry into Greater Pittsburgh Multilist the black brokers have

54

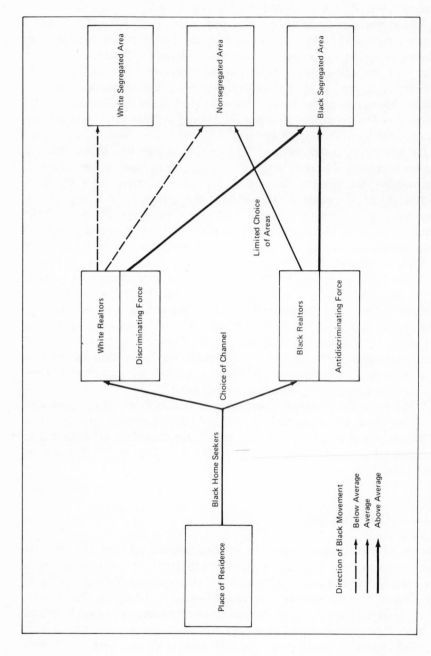

Figure 4-1. A Realty Model of the Channel and Directions of Black Spatial Mobility via Segregated Real Estate Organization

become the most powerful antidiscriminating force available to blacks in the area of owner housing in Pittsburgh.[44] In rental housing they are less effective, since landlords continue to turn down black apartment seekers.

Since the past direction of black movement has been below average to the white segregated areas and above average to the black segregated areas, in order for significant decreases in residential segregation to occur, the pattern of direction must be reversed. Black membership in Multilist has finally made such a reversal possible in owner housing.[45] Some change in direction of black movement is already evident, as illustrated in Figure 4-2. For example, since entry into Multilist in 1967, Lavelle Real Estate, Inc., which sells an average of forty homes per year, has sold on the average the following number of homes per year in white segregated areas of Pittsburgh: three in Point Breeze, six in Squirrel Hill, five in Beechview, and one in Oakland. Lavelle has sold approximately an equal number of homes in white suburban areas, ten per year in Monroeville and eight in Penn Hills.[46]

Oliver Jackson, who has an office in Homewood, became a member of Multilist in June of 1971. Since his entry into the organization, there has been a slight change in the location of homes purchased by blacks through his office. Like Lavelle, he sells an average of 40 homes per year. About 75 percent of the homes sold within the city of Pittsburgh have been in Point Breeze, Bloomfield, East Liberty, or Homewood. The former two communities, are white areas. Jackson has also noticed a trend for black homeowners to locate in suburban Pittsburgh. His office has sold a substantial number of homes in Penn Hills, Monroeville, and Wilkinsburg.[47]

In summary, in the area of owner housing, black real-estate brokers have become the most powerful antidiscriminating force in Pittsburgh. Their impact on the decrease in residential segregation has been felt only since 1967. However, the degree of decrease in segregation in the future will be largely a reflection of the degree to which black home seekers make use of the black real estate broker as a channel for spatial mobility.

Black Financial Institutions

Because nearly all housing is acquired through mortgage credit, mortgage lending institutions play a key role in determining the range of housing choice. Unfortunately, Pittsburgh has only one black owned and operated financial institution engaged in mortgage lending. This is Dwelling House Savings and Loan Association in the Hill District, an organization with assets of $2.9 million.[48] It is one of forty black owned and operated savings and loan associations in the United States. Together these forty institutions have assets of $322 million.

Prior to 1970, Dwelling House Savings and Loan Association issued only 132

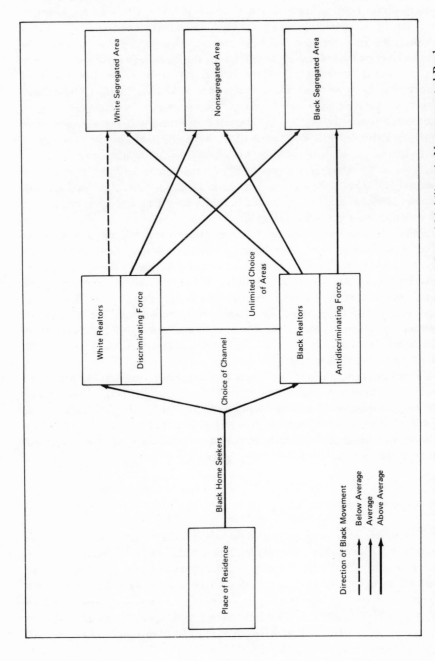

Figure 4-2. A Realty Model of the Channel and Directions of Black Spatial Mobility via Nonsegregated Real Estate Organization

mortgages, but it issued 55 new mortgages in the six months from May to November of 1970. All were FHA or VA insured.[49] In 1971, it made 73 mortgage loans, of which all but one were to blacks. The lone exception was a white divorcee with six children on public assistance, who had been turned down by other banks and savings and loan companies.

The fact that only one mortgage lending institution in Pittsburgh is black owned and operated reflects the scarcity of a potentially very important force against discrimination. Even with the recent increases in its mortgage activity, this institution cannot alone perform more than a minor role in eliminating residential segregation.

Summary and Conclusions

This chapter has demonstrated that a major cause of racial residential segregation in Pittsburgh is racial discrimination in housing. Two opposing groups of forces have been identified: forces operating to segregate residential areas on the basis of race (discriminating forces) and forces operating to desegregate residential areas (antidiscriminating forces).

Although the discriminating forces have been in operation all along, detailed data on their workings did not become available until 1959. Most of these forces operate primarily by actions that directly prevent black home seekers from obtaining housing in white areas or deter them from looking in these areas. The exception is white real estate organizations, which operate to maintain a segregated white real estate system by denying black brokers membership and thus barring them from selling properties in all areas of the city. The intensity of operation of the discriminating forces was not evenly distributed throughout the city; complaints of discriminatory behavior occurred mainly in areas near large black communities. This does not seem to indicate that these areas are more discriminatory than others, but rather that more blacks seek housing in these areas than elsewhere.

The antidiscriminatory forces—i.e., those forces working to decrease residential segregation—began to be effective only in the 1960s.[50] They played a role in the slight decline in residential segregation from 1960 to 1970. However, the discriminating forces are more powerful and have been in operation much longer. It is these forces which explain the high level of residential segregation that cannot be explained by housing cost inequality.

Notes

1. JONES v. MAYER, 392 (U.S.), 409 (1968).
2. The Supreme Court declared that restrictive covenants designed to

prevent the sale or resale of real property to persons of specified race, color, religion, national origin, or ancestry are unenforceable by either State or Federal courts, on the grounds that such enforcement would constitute governmental action in furtherance of racial discrimination. See SHELLY v. KRAEMER, 334 (U.S.) 1 (1948) and HURD v. HODGE, 334 (U.S.) 24 (1948). In denying enforceability of racially restrictive covenants, however, the Supreme Court did not specify that they (racially restrictive covenants) were illegal or void.

3. United States Federal Housing Administration, UNDERWRITING MANUAL (Washington, D.C.: United States Government Printing Office, 1938), par. 937.

4. United States Federal Housing Administration, UNDERWRITING MANUAL (Washington, D.C.: United States Government Printing Office, 1947), par. 1320.

5. For the purpose of this study, a real estate broker means any person, partnership, association, or corporation licensed by the State of Pennsylvania Real Estate Commission, who for a fee, commission, or other consideration sells, exchanges, purchases, rents, or leases or can negotiate the sale, exchange, purchase, rental, or leasing of any real property, i.e., houses, apartments, and lots. A real estate salesman is any person, partnership, association, or corporation associated with a licensed real estate broker to perform any function of a real estate broker.

6. Pittsburgh Commission on Human Relations, Report of the Commission, A SURVEY OF PITTSBURGH REALTORS (Pittsburgh, 1965), pp. i-ii.

7. Pittsburgh Commission on Human Relations, Report of the Commission, 1967 RE-SURVEY OF PITTSBURGH REALTORS (Pittsburgh, 1967), p. 9.

8. Ibid., p. 13.

9. See: Rose Helper, RACIAL POLICIES AND PRACTICES OF REAL ESTATE BROKERS (Minneapolis: University of Minnesota Press, 1969), p. 24; and Stuart H. Palmer, "The Role of the Real Estate Agent in the Structuring of Residential Areas: A Study in Social Control" (Unpublished Ph.D. dissertation, Yale University, 1955).

10. Deborah M. Elliott and Barbara F. Gluckman, "The Impact of the Pittsburgh Fair Housing Ordinance: A Pilot Study," THE JOURNAL OF INTERGROUP RELATIONS 5 (Autumn, 1966): 81, 84.

11. By high-income areas is meant areas classified in the first Quartile; that is, those census tracts with the highest obtainable scores on the Urban Level of Living Index. The index score comprised seven socioeconomic variables; the composite score for each census tract or area is the accumulated percentage obtained on each of the seven variables. For a detailed discussion and explanation of the Level of Living Index see, Health and Welfare Association of Allegheny County, URBAN-LEVEL-OF-LIVING INDEX, Technical Bulletin No. 9 (Pittsburgh: Department of City Planning, June 1964), p. 2.

12. Louis Mason, Jr., "The Pittsburgh Fair Housing Law—Six Years Later."

(Mimeographed text of testimony presented before the City Council of Baltimore, May 18, 1965), pp. 6-7.

13. Helper, RACIAL POLICIES AND PRACTICES OF REAL ESTATE BROKERS, p. 32; the economic motive for discrimination has also been discussed by others; see Gary S. Becker, THE ECONOMICS OF DISCRIMINATION (Chicago: University of Chicago Press, 1957), p. 59; and Richard F. Muth, CITIES AND HOUSING: THE SPATIAL PATTERN OF URBAN LAND USE (Chicago: University of Chicago Press, 1969).

14. Greater Pittsburgh Board of Realtors, "1965 Statement of Policy," REAL ESTATE 13 (March 1965): 7.

15. Ibid.

16. Other researchers have arrived at similar conclusions. See Herman H. Long and Charles H. Johnson, PEOPLE VS. PROPERTY: RACE RESTRICTIVE COVENANTS IN HOUSING (Nashville, Tenn.: Fisk University Press, 1947), pp. 56-58; Robert C. Weaver, THE NEGRO GHETTO (New York: Harcourt, 1948), pp. ix and 215; also Charles Abrams, FORBIDDEN NEIGHBORS—A STUDY OF PREJUDICE IN HOUSING (New York: Harper, 1955), p. 158; and Donald S. Frey, "Freedom of Residence in Illinois," CHICAGO BAR RECORD 41 (October 1959): 9-21. In Ohio, white real estate brokers and salesmen have refused outright to show houses to blacks in all-white areas and consistently discourage them from making purchases except in specified areas. See Ohio Civil Rights Commission, A SURVEY OF DISCRIMINATION IN HOUSING IN OHIO (Columbus: Ohio Civil Rights Commission, January 1963), pp. 21-23; also Helper, RACIAL POLICIES AND PRACTICES OF REAL ESTATE BROKERS, pp. 288-92; and U.S., Commission on Civil Rights, CIVIL RIGHTS '63 (Washington, D.C.: Government Printing Office, 1963), p. 162.

17. Robert R. Lavelle, Real Estate Broker, private interview, Pittsburgh, Pa., August 25, 1971.

18. The account of this case is based on the above interview and on ROBERT R. LAVELLE V. THE GREATER PITTSBURGH MULTILIST, INC., AND P.J. RICCA, 422 U.S. 1 (1967). Quotations from Lavelle's correspondence with Multilist are from the latter.

19. By-Laws of the Greater East-End Multilist, Inc., Pittsburgh, May 1, 1963 (revised August 1, 1965), p. 2. (Mimeographed)

20. By "conspiracy," in the law, is meant a combination or confederacy between two or more persons formed for the purpose of committing, by their joint efforts, some unlawful or criminal act, or some act which is innocent in itself, but becomes unlawful when done by the concerted action of the conspirators, or for the purpose of using criminal or unlawful means to the commission of an act not in itself unlawful. See Black, LAW DICTIONARY 85 (4th ed. 1951).

21. ROBERT R. LAVELLE v. THE GREATER PITTSBURGH MULTILIST, INC.

22. There are at least ten Multilist Organizations in the Pittsburgh Metropolitan Area, but the dominant multiple listing organization and the one which operates within the territory where the black brokers are located is the Greater Pittsburgh Multilist, Inc.

23. Multiple listing in one form or another dates back into the 1880s when the first real estate board members met on certain days and "exchanged" information about their listings. After the turn of the twentieth century, the term "multiple listing" was used and by the 1920s it was widely accepted in the United States.

24. By-Laws of the Greater East-End Multilist, Inc., p. 2.

25. Dollar values in this paragraph appear in ROBERT R. LAVELLE V. THE GREATER PITTSBURGH MULTILIST, INC., p. 5.

26. The Sherman Anti-Trust Act is an act to protect trade and commerce against unlawful restraints and monopolies. See Sherman Act, 15 U.S.C. Sec. 1 (1890).

27. See ROBERT R. LAVELLE v. THE GREATER PITTSBURGH MULTILIST, INC., p. 2.

28. The practice of excluding black brokers from membership in white real estate organizations is a common practice in several cities in the United States. See Helper, RACIAL POLICIES AND PRACTICES OF REAL ESTATE BROKERS, pp. 236-37.

29. The following case is typical. See "Landlord Fined in Housing Court," PITTSBURGH HUMAN RELATIONS REVIEW, Fall, 1970, p. 3. In this case, the magistrate concluded that *all* evidence and testimony indicated that discrimination on the basis of race was present. See also Elliott and Gluckman, "Impact of the Pittsburgh Fair Housing Ordinance," p. 81.

30. "Racism" is any attitude, action, or institutional structure which subordinates a person or group because of his or their color. By "institutional structure" is meant any well established, habitual, or widely accepted pattern of action or organizational arrangement, whether formal or informal. For example, the residential segregation of the majority of blacks in Pittsburgh and other large cities is an "institutional structure." See, U.S. Commission on Civil Rights, RACISM IN AMERICA AND HOW TO COMBAT IT (Washington, D.C.: Government Printing Office, 1970), p. 5.

31. U.S., Commission on Civil Rights, HOUSING (Washington, D.C.: Government Printing Office, 1961), p. 29; see also U.S. Commission on Civil Rights, REPORT OF THE COMMISSION, FEDERAL CIVIL RIGHTS ENFORCEMENT EFFORT (Washington, D.C.: Government Printing Office, 1970), p. 512; also Helper, RACIAL POLICIES AND PRACTICES OF REAL ESTATE BROKERS, p. 33.

32. See Elliott and Gluckman, "Impact of the Pittsburgh Fair Housing Ordinance," p. 81.

33. Advance Mortgage Corporation, MIDWESTERN MINORITY HOUSING MARKETS, A Special Report (Pittsburgh: December 1, 1962), p. 28.

34. PITTSBURGH PRESS, June 2, 1959.

35. PITTSBURGH SUN-TELEGRAPH, June 7, 1959.

36. PITTSBURGH PRESS, June 16, 1963.

37. Prior to 1959, the Commission had no power other than that of investigating any and all conditions having an adverse effect upon intergroup relations. See Mason, "The Pittsburgh Fair Housing Law—Six Years Later," pp. 2-3.

38. The Fair Housing Ordinance was actually passed by City Council on December 7, 1958. See Pittsburgh, ORDINANCE NO. 523 (1958). Its effective date was postponed at the request of the Commission on Human Relations.

39. Pittsburgh, Ordinance No. 523 (1958).

40. Pittsburgh Commission on Human Relations, 1967 ANNUAL REPORT (Pittsburgh: 1967), p. 4.

41. Pittsburgh, ORDINANCE NO. 75 (1967).

42. Pittsburgh Commission on Human Relations, 1967 ANNUAL REPORT, p. 2.

43. In reality the Pittsburgh Commission on Human Relations has been little more than a force of "pacification" rather than a significant antidiscriminatory force. Similar comments on the ineffectiveness of the Fair Housing Law were made by Elliott and Gluckman, "Impact of the Pittsburgh Fair Housing Ordinance," p. 85.

44. During the month of August, 1971, eight black brokers or approximately 75 percent of the black brokers of Pittsburgh were interviewed. A common consensus was as follows. Little or no discrimination would exist in the area of "house sells" if black home seekers would make use of black brokers who are members of Multilist. Multilist makes it possible for a black real estate broker to sell any house, whether or not it is listed in a white area. Apparently not enough blacks are taking full advantage of the black brokers. (Pittsburgh, interviews, with selected black real estate brokers, August 1971.) The black brokers concede to the fact that in the area of rental housing, they have little power.

45. This statement, however, is based on the assumption that discrimination by white mortgage lending institutions will continue to decline. Recent action by four federal regulatory agencies lends credibility to this assumption, see: "Rules Proposed to Curb Racial Discrimination by Banks and S & Ls," WALL STREET JOURNAL, December 20, 1971, p. 7.

46. Milton Holt, Real Estate Sales Manager of Lavelle Real Estate, Inc., interview, Pittsburgh, Pa., April 19, 1972.

47. Oliver Jackson, Real Estate Broker, interview, Pittsburgh, Pa., April 14, 1972.

48. See Al Donalson, "Hill Bankers Stake Black Power," PITTSBURGH PRESS, February 6, 1972, p. 10.

49. See Jack Markowitz, "A Lift to Black Home Ownership," PITTSBURGH POST-GAZETTE, November 30, 1970, p. 31.

50. The decade of the sixties appeared to be a major turning point with

respect to legislation related to racial discrimination. Virtually all of the antidiscrimination legislation on the local, state and national levels occurred during the sixties. Pittsburgh led the way with the Fair Housing Law of 1958 (amended in 1967), followed by the Pennsylvania Civil Rights Act of 1961, and Executive Order 11063 of 1962 and culminating with Titles VI and VIII of the U.S. Civil Rights Acts of 1964 and 1968 respectively.

5 Conclusions

This study was designed to test the following hypotheses: (1) that the residential segregation of Afro-Americans in Pittsburgh (a) remained at a high level between 1930 and 1970 and (b) increased continuously over that period; and (2) that the high level of residential segregation in Pittsburgh has been caused not by housing cost inequality, but by racial discrimination in housing.

Hypothesis (1a) is clearly confirmed by the study. Segregation was defined as being at a "high level" if it exceeded 50 percent as measured by the Gini index explained in Chapter 1, and from 1930 to 1970, Afro-Americans in Pittsburgh were found to have remained from 70.5 to 75.7 percent segregated.

The study disproves hypothesis (1b). During the four decades there were both increases and decreases in the amount of residential segregation. From 1930 to 1940 there was an increase in segregation of 3.3 percentage points, changing the level of segregation from 71.6 percent in 1930 to 74.9 percent in 1940. From 1940 to 1950 there was another increase of 0.8 percentage points, increasing the amount of segregation to 75.7 percent, the highest level reached during the four decades. After 1950 the trend became one of slight decreases. There was a 2.8 percentage point decrease from 1950 to 1960 and a 2.4 percentage point decrease from 1960 to 1970.

Considerable change in residential segregation by census tract occurred from 1930 to 1970. From 1930 to 1960, the most segregated census tracts in the city were located in the Hill District Community. However by 1970 the most segregated tracts were in Homewood-Brushton. Intratract racial change occurred in all six possible directions over the forty year period; that is, there were changes of tracts from black segregated to white segregated, black segregated to nonsegregated, white segregated to black segregated, white segregated to non-segregated, nonsegregated to black segregated, and nonsegregated to white segregated. However, racial change occurred only in those tracts that were less than one percent segregated to begin with. Whether this apparent one percent limit is unique to Pittsburgh or also holds true for other American cities requires comparative study of racial change in several cities. No attempt at generalizing will be made here.

The study fully substantiates hypothesis (2). First, it shows that the high level of Afro-American residential segregation from 1940 to 1970 cannot be attributed to housing cost inequality between blacks and whites. Statistically, the housing cost factor could explain only the following proportions of residential segregation in each decade: 7 percent in 1940, leaving 93 percent unexplained;

18 percent in 1950, leaving 82 percent unexplained; 16 percent in 1960, leaving 84 percent unexplained; and 15 percent in 1970, leaving 85 percent unexplained. Thus, by far the greater part of the observed level of segregation requires an explanation other than housing cost.

The findings clearly indicate that no matter how much the blacks of Pittsburgh pay for the purchase or rental of their homes, location outside of black segregated census tracts is rare. Likewise, no matter how little the whites of Pittsburgh pays for housing, they seldom share residental location with blacks.[1] Thus, upward economic mobility by the blacks of Pittsburgh is no guarantee of spatial mobility, that is, freedom to move into the residential area of one's choice subject only to ability to pay and without other restrictions or limitations.

In spite of the evidence presented in this study, there are those who would argue that blacks do in fact have spatial mobility and that blacks who remain in black segregated areas are there by choice. It is conceivable that some blacks might desire to live only with other blacks even if they had total freedom to choose their living space. The explanation for their preferences, however, cannot be totally divorced from past and present forces of racism and discrimination. Since blacks have never had the total freedom to live in any area of the city of Pittsburgh, the influence of personal preference cannot be adequately measured, and no measurement was attempted in this study. The case for personal preference as a factor in racial residential segregation remains hypothetical. There is evidence that those who advance such arguments as "blacks prefer to live among their own kind" do so in an attempt to maintain the status quo and prevent or delay any efforts towards decreasing residential segregation and eliminating the ghetto.[2]

This study is further evidence that any attempt to explain the high level of Afro-American residential segregation found in most American cities by examining only factors of racial economic inequality is an exercise in futility. In other words, the primary cause of Afro-American residential segregation is racism or racial discrimination, not racial economic inequality.

The magnitude of racial discrimination in housing in Pittsburgh has been a function of two opposing groups of forces: discriminating forces, which operate to segregate residential areas on the basis of race, and antidiscriminating forces, which operate to desegregate them. This study identifies six major discriminating forces: white real estate brokers and salesmen, white real estate organizations, white owners, white financial institutions, white newspapers, and white home builders. It identifies three antidiscriminating forces: the Pittsburgh Commission on Human Relations, black real estate brokers and salesmen, and black financial institutions.

The white real estate brokers, salesmen, and business organizations are the strongest of the discriminating forces. Their motives appear to be largely economic; once property gets into black hands, they do not expect to be able to regain control of it. They use such discriminating techinques as failure to process the application of blacks and maintenance of separate rental lists. The most effective technique used by the real estate organizations (Multilist) until recently was to refuse membership to black brokers, thus barring them from selling properties in much of the city. The discriminating forces were most active in areas adjacent to sizeable black communities. For example, Oakland-Shadyside, which is located very close to two of the largest black communities in Pittsburgh (the Hill District and Homewood-Brushton) accounted for 27.9 percent of the total complaints of racial discrimination from 1959 to 1970. The lower percentages of complaints in areas not adjacent to black communities reflect the fact that fewer blacks seek housing in those areas in the first place.

The discriminating forces were virtually unopposed until the 1960s, and the antidiscriminating forces still do not equal them in strength. The role of the Commission on Human Relations is weakened by the mildness of penalties under Pittsburgh's fair housing ordinance, and the fact that the city has only one black owned institution making mortgage loans limits the effectiveness of this potential force against discrimination. The most promising of the antidiscriminating forces consists of black real estate brokers, who have finally, through court action, obtained membership in formerly all-white real-estate organizations.

If racial residential segregation is to be substantially reduced from its present high level, the antidiscriminating forces must be better equipped to deal with the forces of discrimination. While there have been slight decreases in residential segregation since 1950, these have not been significant, and the actions of antidiscriminating forces do not seem to have greatly accelerated the process. The discriminating forces are still very influential, perhaps reflecting in part their ability to adapt to changes in laws by reverting to subtle rather than overt behavior. The following changes are urgently needed in Pittsburgh: (1) The Pittsburgh Commission on Human Relations must be granted the power to inflict economic penalties for discrimination that outweigh its economic advantages. An example of a penalty that should be introduced is to revoke the license of the broker and financial institution that is found guilty of discrimination. (2) More black mortgage lending institutions must be established, with the ability to grant loans to any and all black home seekers. Movement in these directions should lead to real progress in reducing racial residential segregation.

Notes

1. Taeuber used the same variables—i.e., value for owner-occupied units and rent for renter-occupied units—and derived similar conclusions for fifteen cities. See Karl E. Taeuber, "Residential Segregation," SCIENTIFIC AMERICAN 213 (1965), p. 19.

2. See David A. Wallace, "Residential Concentration of Negroes in Chicago" (unpublished Ph.D. dissertation, Harvard University, 1953), p. 25; also Gunnar Myrdal, AN AMERICAN DILEMMA (New York: Harper and Brothers, 1944), pp. 619-621.

Appendix A
Measurement of Segregation Among Selected Census Tracts of Pittsburgh, 1970

Tract	Whites as Percent of Total White[a] (x_i)	Percent Racial Deficit $(x_i\text{-}y_i)$	Blacks as Percent of Total Black[b] (y_i)
0704[c]	0.27	0.0	0.27
0102[d]	0.83	0.24	0.59
0504[e]	0.04	2.93	2.97

[a]Total White = 412,280
[b]Total Black = 104,904
[c]Nonsegregated tract
[d]White segregated tract
[e]Black segregated tract

	Census Tract Data		
Tract	Number White	Number Black	Percent Black
0704	1111	287	20.4
0102	3432	620	15.2
0504	161	3120	94.6

Appendix B
Census Tracts Experiencing Racial Change, 1930-1970

Tract Number	Percent Racial Deficit 1930	1930 Number White	Number Black	Percent Black	Number White	1940 Number Black	Percent Black
11-F	0.01	1439	133	8.4	1529	143	8.6
10-B	0.03	1086	112	9.3	1298	52	3.9
28-A	0.06	1340	154	10.3	1435	123	7.9
2-D	0.09	1930	222	10.3	1080	107	8.9
4-A	0.57	2412	527	17.9	2234	176	7.3
20-K	0.02	528	58	9.9	407	43	9.6
5-F	0.56	609	351	37.2	71	6	9.0
21-B	0.01	4545	402	8.1	4258	538	11.2
10-E	0.03	225	6	2.5	197	34	14.7
11-E	0.05	228	0	0.0	242	29	10.7
13-D	0.09	5859	474	7.5	5326	639	10.7
11-A	0.01	39	0	0.0	27	2	8.0
7-D	0.00	1704	151	8.2	1743	170	8.9

Appendix B (cont.)

Tract Number	Percent Racial Deficit 1940	1940 Number White	Number Black	Percent Black	Number White	1950 Number Black	Percent Black
11-E	0.01	242	29	10.7	260	11	4.1
20-J	0.01	1746	186	9.6	2202	211	8.7
10-E	0.02	197	34	14.7	1075	0	0.0
26-H	0.06	3783	350	8.5	3448	779	18.4
4-A	0.08	2234	176	7.3	3718	1744	31.9
5-F	0.00	71	7	9.8	1328	1205	47.6
20-K	0.00	407	43	10.5	870	20	2.2

Tract Number	Percent Racial Deficit 1950	1950 Number White	Number Black	Percent Black	Number White	1960 Number Black	Percent Black
22-F[a]	0.03	728	124	14.6	1083	95	8.1
8-H	0.21	2153	470	17.9	1572	273	14.8
2-B	0.09	996	209	17.3	924	176	16.0
2-D[b]	0.01	754	96	11.3	559	326	36.8
12-H	0.01	1747	238	12.0	656	985	60.0
12-G	0.06	2156	253	10.5	692	1471	68.0
20-I	0.06	964	87	8.3	673	185	21.6
22-C	0.21	1818	76	4.0	1178	285	19.5
4-H	0.31	2958	154	4.9	2578	1741	40.3
11-A[c]	0.00	12	0	0.0	3730	20	0.5

[a]Minor boundary change and tract number change to 22-I in 1960.
[b]Minor boundary change and tract number change to 2-F in 1960.
[c]Minor boundary change and tract number change to 11-K in 1960.

Appendix B (cont.)

Tract Number	Percent Racial Deficit 1960	1960 Number White	Number Black	Percent Black	Number White	1970 Number Black	Percent Black
31-C	0.05	884	221	20.0	1161	115	8.9
7-G	0.05	1291	298	18.8	639	87	12.0
3-F	0.07	141	94	40.0	671	58	7.9
6-E	0.24	1410	507	26.4	1107	247	18.2
11-M	0.65	1944	1026	34.5	1028	212	16.9
21-G	0.60	2177	1018	31.9	7	0	0.0
26-N	0.08	515	12	2.3	1242	3304	72.4
4-I	0.10	2094	291	12.2	1554	491	23.5
25-C	0.15	2136	252	10.6	725	1061	59.2
12-A	0.17	2404	285	10.6	1432	880	38.0
21-C	0.25	1618	56	3.3	865	475	35.4
10-FB	0.26	4383	562	11.4	3098	977	23.9
14-E	0.47	3379	170	4.8	2317	800	25.5
11-H	0.59	3974	153	3.7	2842	970	25.3
7-D	0.10	1518	188	11.0	1111	287	20.4

Selected Bibliography

Books

Abrams, Charles. FORBIDDEN NEIGHBORS: A STUDY OF PREJUDICE IN HOUSING. New York: Harper and Brothers, 1955.
Bachi, Roberto. STATISTICAL ANALYSIS OF GEOGRAPHICAL SERIES. Jerusalem: Hebrew University and Israel Central Bureau of Statistics, 1957.
Becker, Gary S. THE ECONOMICS OF DISCRIMINATION. Chicago: University of Chicago Press, 1957.
Dixon, J.W. ed. BIOMEDICAL COMPUTER PROGRAMS. Berkeley: University of California Press, 1968.
Doyle, Bertram. THE ETIQUETTE OF RACE RELATIONS IN THE SOUTH. Chicago: University of Chicago Press, 1937.
Drake, St. Clair, and Cayton, Horace R. BLACK METROPOLIS: A STUDY OF NEGRO LIFE IN A NORTHERN CITY. New York: Harcourt, Brace, 1945.
Duncan, Otis D., Cuzzort, Ray P., and Duncan, Beverly. THE NEGRO POPULATION OF CHICAGO: A STUDY OF RESIDENTIAL SUCCESSION. Chicago: University of Chicago Press, 1957.
Duncan, Otis D., and Duncan, Beverly. STATISTICAL GEOGRAPHY. Glencoe, Illinois: The Free Press, 1961.
Epstein, Abraham. THE NEGRO MIGRANT IN PITTSBURGH. Pittsburgh: University of Pittsburgh Press, 1918.
Frieden, Bernard. THE FUTURE OF OLD NEIGHBORHOODS. Cambridge: MIT Press, 1964.
Hawley, Amos. HUMAN ECOLOGY. New York: The Ronald Press, 1950.
Health and Welfare Association of Allegheny County. URBAN-LEVEL-OF-LIVING INDEX. Technical Bulletin No. 9. Pittsburgh: Department of City Planning, June 1964.
Helper, Rose. RACIAL POLICIES AND PRACTICES OF REAL ESTATE BROKERS. Minneapolis: University of Minnesota Press, 1969.
Isard, Walter. METHODS OF REGIONAL ANALYSIS: AN INTRODUCTION TO REGIONAL SCIENCE. New York: John Wiley and Sons, Inc., 1960.
Kendall, Maurice G. THE ADVANCED THEORY OF STATISTICS. London: Griffin & Co., 3rd ed., 1947.
Laurenti, Luigi. PROPERTY VALUES AND RACE: STUDIES IN SEVEN CITIES. Berkeley: University of California Press, 1960.
Liberson, Stanley. ETHNIC PATTERNS IN AMERICAN CITIES. New York: The Free Press of Glencoe, 1963.
Long, Herman H., and Johnson, Charles S. PEOPLE VS. PROPERTY: RACE RESTRICTIVE CONVENANTS IN HOUSING. Nashville: Fisk University Press, 1947.

McIntire, David. RESIDENCE AND RACE. Berkeley: University of California Press, 1960.

Muth, Richard F. CITIES AND HOUSING: THE SPATIAL PATTERN OF URBAN LAND USE. Chicago: University of Chicago Press, 1969.

Myrdal, Gunnar. AN AMERICAN DILEMMA. 2 vols. New York: Harper and Brothers, 1944.

Rose, Harold M. SOCIAL PROCESSES IN THE CITY: RACE AND URBAN RESIDENTIAL CHOICE. Commission on College Geography, Resource Paper #6. Washington, D.C.: Association of American Geographers, 1969.

Rose, Peter. THEY AND WE. New York: Random House, 1964.

Scott, Barbara. THE STATUS OF HOUSING OF NEGROES IN PITTSBURGH. Pittsburgh: Pittsburgh Commission on Human Relations, 1962.

Taeuber, Karl E., and Taeuber, Alma F. NEGROES IN CITIES: RESIDENTIAL SEGREGATION AND NEIGHBORHOOD CHANGE. Chicago: Aldine Publishing Co., 1965.

Weaver, Robert C. THE NEGRO GHETTO. New York: Harcourt, Brace, 1948.

Witchen, Elsie. TUBERCULOSIS AND THE NEGRO IN PITTSBURGH. Pittsburgh: Tuberculosis League of Pittsburgh, 1934.

Wright, Richard. THE NEGRO IN PENNSLYVANIA. Philadelphia: A.M.E. Book Concern Printers, 1909.

Articles

Beehler, George Jr., "Colored Occupancy Raises Values." THE REVIEW OF THE SOCIETY OF RESIDENTIAL APPRAISERS (September 1945): 3-4.

Bell, Wendell and Willis, Ernest M. "The Segregation of Negroes in American Cities." ANNALS OF THE AMERICAN ACADEMY OF POLITICAL AND SOCIAL SCIENCE, 140 (November 1928): 105-115.

Burgess, Ernest W. "The Growth of the City: An Introduction to a Research Project." In THE CITY. Edited by Robert E. Park, Ernest W. Burgess, and Roderick D. McKenzie. Chicago: University of Chicago Press, 1925: 47-62.

_____. "Residential Segregation in American Cities." ANNALS OF THE AMERICAN ACADEMY OF POLITICAL AND SOCIAL SCIENCE, Publication No. 2180 (November, 1928), pp. 1-11.

Cowgill, Donald O. and Cowgill, Mary. "An Index of Segregation Based on Block Statistics." AMERICAN SOCIOLOGICAL REVIEW 16 (December 1957): 831-835.

Donalson, Al. "Hill Bankers Stake Black Power." PITTSBURGH PRESS, February 6, 1972.

Duncan, Otis D. and Duncan, Beverly. "A Methodological Analysis of Segregation Indices." AMERICAN SOCIOLOGICAL REVIEW 20 (April 1955): 210-217.

Elliott, Deborah M., and Gluckman, Barbara F. "The Impact of the Pittsburgh Fair Housing Ordinance: A Pilot Study." THE JOURNAL OF INTERGROUP RELATIONS 5 (Autumn, 1966): 75-85.

Foley, Donald L. "Census Tracts and Urban Research." JOURNAL OF THE AMERICAN STATISTICAL ASSOCIATION 43 (December 1953): 733-742.

Frey, Donald S. "Freedom of Residence in Illinois." CHICAGO BAR RECORD 41 (October 1959): 9-21.

Gibbs, Jack P. "Some Measures of the Spatial Distribution and Redistribution of Urban Phenomena." In URBAN RESEARCH METHODS. Edited by Jack P. Gibbs. Princeton: D. Van Nostrand Co., Inc., 1961: 235-252.

Greater Pittsburgh Board of Realtors. "1965 Statement of Policy." REAL ESTATE 13 (March 1965): 7.

Hillery, G.A. "Definitions of Community: Areas of Agreement." RURAL SOCIOLOGY 20 (1955): 111-123.

Hoover, Edgar M. "The Measurement of Industrial Localization." REVIEW OF ECONOMICS AND STATISTICS 18 (November 1936): 162-171.

Jahn, Julius A., Schmid, Calvin F., and Schrag, Clarence. "The Measurement of Ecological Segregation." AMERICAN SOCIOLOGICAL REVIEW 20 (April 1955): 210-217.

Kantrowitz, Nathan. "Ethnic and Racial Segregation in the New York Metropolis, 1960." AMERICAN JOURNAL OF SOCIOLOGY 74 (1969): 685-695.

"Landlord Fined in Housing Court." PITTSBURGH HUMAN RELATIONS REVIEW. Fall, 1970: 3.

Langendorf, Richard. "Residential Desegregation Potential." JOURNAL OF THE AMERICAN INSTITUTE OF PLANNERS 35 March 1969, pp. 90-95.

Lieberson, Stanley. "The Impact of Residential Segregation on Ethnic Assimilation." SOCIAL FORCES 40 (October 1961): 52-57.

Lorenz, O.M. "Methods of Measuring the Concentration of Wealth." PUBLICATIONS OF THE AMERICAN STATISTICAL ASSOCIATION, New Series, Vol. 9 (1904-1905): 209-219.

Markowitz, Jack. "A Lift to Black Home Ownership." PITTSBURGH POST-GAZETTE. November 30, 1970.

Moron, Alonzo G., and Stephen, F.F. "The Negro Population in Pittsburgh and Allegheny County." THE SOCIAL RESEARCH BULLETIN 1 (April 20, 1933): 1-5.

Morrill, Richard. "The Negro Ghetto: Problems and Alternatives." GEOGRAPHICAL REVIEW 55 (1965): 339-361.

Rapkin, Chester. "Price Discrimination Against Negroes in the Rental Housing Market." In ESSAYS IN URBAN LAND ECONOMICS. Los Angeles: University of California Real Estate Research Program, 1966, pp. 333-345.

Rose, Harold M. "The Development of an Urban Subsystem: The Case of the Negro Ghetto." ANNALS OF THE ASSOCIATION OF AMERICAN GEOGRAPHERS 60 (1970): 1-17.

"Rules Proposed to Curb Racial Discrimination by Banks and S & Ls." WALL STREET JOURNAL, December 20, 1971.

Taeuber, Karl E. "The Effect of Income Redistribution on Racial Residential Segregation." URBAN AFFAIRS QUARTERLY 4 (September 1968): 5-14.

_____. "Negro Residential Segregation: Trends and Measurement." SOCIAL PROBLEMS 12 (Summer, 1964): 42-50.

_____. "Residential Segregation." SCIENTIFIC AMERICAN 213 (August 1965): 12-19.

Williams, Josephine. "Another Commentary on the So-Called Segregation Indices." AMERICAN SOCIOLOGICAL REVIEW 13 (June 1948): 298-303.

Wright, John K. "Some Measures of Distribution." ANNALS OF THE ASSOCIATION OF AMERICAN GEOGRAPHERS 27 (December 1937): 137-211.

Theses and Dissertations

Helper, Rose. "The Racial Practices of Real Estate Institutions in Selected Areas of Chicago." Unpublished Ph.D. dissertation. University of Chicago, 1958.

Lee, Douglas B. "Analysis and Description of Residential Segregation." Unpublished M.A. thesis. Cornell University, 1966.

Moron, Alonzo G. "Distribution of the Negro Population in Pittsburgh, 1910-1930." Unpublished M.A. thesis. University of Pittsburgh, 1935.

Palmer, Stuart H. "The Role of the Real Estate Agent in the Structuring of Residential Areas: A Study in Social Control." Unpublished Ph.D. dissertation. Yale University, 1955.

Rathwell, John N. "Status of Pittsburgh Negores in Regard to Origin, Length of Residence, and Economic Aspects of Their Life." Unpublished M.A. thesis. University of Pittsburgh, 1935.

Rosenbloom, Miriam. "An Outline of the History of the Negro in the Pittsburgh Area." Unpublished M.A. thesis. University of Pittsburgh, 1945.

Taeuber, Alma F. "Comparative Urban Analysis of Negro Residential Succession." Unpublished Ph.D. dissertation. University of Chicago, 1962.

Wallace, David A. "Residential Concentration of Negroes in Chicago." Unpublished Ph.D. dissertation. Harvard University, 1953.

Wilkins, Arthur H. "The Residential Distribution of Occupational Groups in Eight Cities of the United States in 1950." Unpublished Ph.D. dissertation. University of Chicago, 1956.

Woolfe, Jacqueline W. "The Changing Pattern of Residence of the Negro in Pittsburgh, Pennsylvania, With Emphasis on the Period 1930-1960." Unpublished M.A. thesis. University of Pittsburgh, 1962.

Other Unpublished Material

Berry, Brian J., et al. "Down From the Summit." Unpublished Paper. Center for Urban Studies, University of Chicago, 1969.

By-Laws of the Greater East-End Multilist, Inc. Pittsburgh, May 1, 1963 (revised August 1, 1965). Mimeographed.

Mason, Louis, Jr., "The Pittsburgh Fair Housing Law—Six Years Later." Text of Testimony presented before the City Council of Baltimore. May 18, 1965. Mimeographed.

Zelder, Raymond E. "Racial Segregation in Urban Housing Markets." Unpublished Paper. Center for Urban Studies. University of Chicago, 1969.

Public Documents

U.S. Department of Commerce. Bureau of the Census. SIXTEENTH CENSUS OF THE UNITED STATES, 1940: POPULATION AND HOUSING, Vol. 7, STATISTICS FOR CENSUS TRACTS, Pittsburgh.

_____. UNITED STATES CENSUS OF POPULATION: 1950, Vol. 3, CENSUS TRACT STATISTICS, Pittsburgh.

_____. UNITED STATES CENSUS OF POPULATION: 1960, Vol. 1, CHARACTERISTICS OF THE POPULATION: CENSUS TRACTS, Pittsburgh.

_____. UNITED STATES CENSUS OF HOUSING: 1970, Advance Report, GENERAL HOUSING CHARACTERISTICS, Pennsylvania.

_____. Federal Housing Administration. UNDERWRITING MANUAL. Washington, D.C.: Government Printing Office, 1938.

_____. Federal Housing Administration. UNDERWRITING MANUAL. Washington, D.C.: Government Printing Office, 1947.

Reports

Advance Mortgage Corporation. MIDWESTERN MINORITY HOUSING MARKETS. A Special Report. Pittsburgh, December 1, 1962.

Commonwealth of Pennsylvania. Department of Welfare. NEGRO SURVEY OF PENNSYLVANIA. A Report of the Department. Harrisburgh, 1928.

Ohio Commission on Civil Rights. A SURVEY OF DISCRIMINATION IN HOUSING IN OHIO. A Report of the Commission. Columbus: Ohio Commission on Civil Rights, January, 1963.

Pittsburgh Commission on Human Relations. A SURVEY OF PITTSBURGH REALTORS. A Report of the Commission. Pittsburgh, 1965.

_____. 1970 ANNUAL REPORT. A Report of the Commission. Pittsburgh, 1970.

Pittsburgh Commission on Human Relations. 1967 RE-SURVEY OF PITTSBURGH REALTORS. A Report of the Commission. Pittsburgh, 1967.

_____. 1967 ANNUAL REPORT. A Report of the Commission. Pittsburgh, 1967.

U.S. Commission on Civil Rights. HOUSING. A Report of the Commission. Washington, D.C.: Government Printing Office, 1961.

_____ . FEDERAL CIVIL RIGHTS ENFORCEMENT EFFORT. A Report of the Commission. Washington, D.C.: Government Printing Office, 1970.

_____ . RACISM IN AMERICA AND HOW TO COMBAT IT. A Report of the Commission. Washington, D.C.: Government Printing Office, 1970.

_____ . CIVIL RIGHTS '63. A Report of the Commission. Washington, D.C.: Government Printing Office, 1963.

Legal Citations

HURD v. HODGE. 334 U.S. 24 (1948).
JONES v. MAYER. 392 U.S. 409 (1968).
LAVELLE v. THE GREATER PITTSBURGH MULTILIST, INC. AND P.J. RICCA. 422 U.S. 1 (1967).
Pittsburgh. ORDINANCE NO. 523 (1958).
_____ . ORDINANCE NO. 75 (1967).
SHERMAN ANTI-TRUST ACT. 15 U.S.C., Sec. 1 (1890).
SKELLEY v. KRAEMER. 334 U.S. 1 (1948).

Other Sources

Pittsburgh, Pennsylvania. Personal interviews with selected real estate brokers. August 1971.

Index

About the Author

Joe T. Darden is an Assistant Professor of Geography and Urban Affairs at Michigan State University. He was graduated from Jackson State College in 1965 and received master's and doctor's degrees at the University of Pittsburgh. From 1971 to 1972 Dr. Darden was a Danforth Foundation Fellow at the University of Chicago. His areas of interest are Urban and Social Geography, with special emphasis on minority groups.